T0270268

WHY
TAMMY
WYNETTE
MATTERS

Music
Matters

Evelyn McDonnell and Oliver Wang

Series Editors

WHY TAMMY WYNETTE MATTERS

Steacy Easton

UNIVERSITY OF TEXAS PRESS

AUSTIN

Requests for permission to reproduce material from this work should be sent to:
    Permissions
    University of Texas Press
    P.O. Box 7819
    Austin, TX 78713-7819
    utpress.utexas.edu/rp-form

♾ The paper used in this book meets the minimum requirements of ANSI/NISO Z39.48-1992 (R1997) (Permanence of Paper).

Library of Congress Cataloging-in-Publication Data

Names: Easton, Steacy, author.
Title: Why Tammy Wynette matters / Steacy Easton.
Description: First edition. | Austin : University of Texas Press, 2023. | Series: Music matters
    Identifiers: LCCN 2022049653
    ISBN 978-1-4773-2464-6 (cloth)
    ISBN 978-1-4773-2750-0 (pdf)
    ISBN 978-1-4773-2751-7 (epub)
Subjects: LCSH: Wynette, Tammy. | Wynette, Tammy — Criticism and interpretation. | Country music — History and criticism | Women country musicians — United States — Biography. | Women singers — United States — Biography. | Country musicians — United States — Biography. | Singers — United States — Biography.
Classification: LCC ML420.W9 E27 2023 | DDC 782.421642092
[B] — dc23/eng/20221102
LC record available at https://lccn.loc.gov/2022049653

doi:10.7560/324646

CONTENTS

INTRODUCTION

This book makes two arguments about the life and work of the artist Tammy Wynette, both of them deeply political but also aesthetic. The first is that Wynette was one of the greatest creators and singers of country music of the twentieth century. The second is that Wynette made her life into her work and that this transformation was itself art. Each of these arguments is complex, and each is unresolved.

Tammy Wynette grew up poor in rural Mississippi, married at seventeen in 1960, and in the process of having three babies and learning to do hair, decided to try to fulfill her dream of becoming a country music singer. While working as a hairdresser, she started singing on television in 1965 for a local show in Birmingham, and after she ended her marriage, she made her way to Nashville with her three young daughters to launch her singing career.

Wynette made the rounds of the recording companies in Nashville and was signed by the producer Billy Sherrill, a fellow Alabamian, in 1966 and in short order had four major singles — "Apartment #9"; "My Elusive Dreams," a duet; "Take Me to Your World"; and "I Don't Wanna Play House" — and started winning awards. In 1967 she married Don Chapel, a songwriter and Nashville insider, and in 1968 and 1969, she released two singles that would cement her reputation for life—"D-I-V-O-R-C-E" and "Stand By Your Man."

There is some question about when Wynette started seeing country star George Jones, and whether she was stepping out on Chapel, but she divorced Chapel in 1968 and married Jones in 1969, and then divorced him by 1975, though they recorded together into the 1980s. The marriage resulted in many legendary songs, including "Two Story House," "Golden Ring," and "(We're Not) The Jet Set," and six albums—and they made three more after their marriage ended. The earliest years would be the apex of her career, resulting in her receiving the Country Music Association Female Vocalist of the Year Award in 1968, 1969, and 1970, among other major awards.[1] Her next marriage, to Michael Tomlin, began in the summer of 1976 and lasted less than six weeks. Her final marriage was in 1978 to George Richey, and this union lasted for the rest of her life. She also spent some of the mid-1970s in an off-and-on relationship with Burt Reynolds, a romantic pairing that became a lifelong friendship.

Wynette's life from the 1970s onward continued in chaos and began a pattern of misfortune and ill health. She reported being kidnapped in 1978, a crime that has yet to be solved. There were dozens of surgeries, including a hysterectomy in the late 1970s. She developed a dependence on prescription opiates and in 1986 went to the Betty Ford Center for treatment. She had one last hit song, with the English jesters the KLF, "Justified and Ancient (Stand By the Jams)," in 1991. In 1993, her album *Honky Tonk Angels*, with Loretta Lynn and Dolly Parton, came out to critical and commercial success, and two years later, she and Jones recorded and toured their last work together.[2] She died under mysterious circumstances on April 6, 1998. Though her death was first blamed on a blood clot, her children had her body disinterred and another autopsy performed, this one concluding she had died of heart failure.[3]

Wynette's marriages were abusive. After a forced commitment and electroconvulsive therapy while married to her first husband, she said in her autobiography she had been hit and chased with a gun by Jones, and there was much speculation that the 1978 kidnapping was faked to distract from Richey's physical abuse (or for publicity). She also endured dozens of incidents of harassment, stalking, and threats in the 1970s, including significant damage to property.[4] Who committed this harassment continues to be a mystery.

Wynette made art out of a difficult life, but her music is genius even if a listener knows nothing about her biography. Her first single, "Apartment #9,"[5] uses the image of a physical location to discuss the failure of a marriage. "Apartment #9" is less than three minutes long and a harrowing example of domestic loneliness. It has everything one expects from a Tammy song—the first-person storytelling, a tight narrative of isolation and loss, a prioritizing of women's pain over men's fecklessness, a voice that catches in the right places, and an arrangement that negotiates a territory between lushness and spareness. It's a song created collectively, written by Fern Foley (Bobby Austin), Fuzzy Owen, and honky-tonk singer Johnny Paycheck and played by pedal-steel player Pete Drake. Bobby Austin recorded the song first,[6] in 1966, but it was Wynette's first single, released the same year, and the one that settled the themes for the rest of her life.[7]

There are other brilliant songs that resound with the

deeply personal from Wynette's life story. "Your Good Girl's Gonna Go Bad," in an ironic reversal, imagines trapping a cheating man by making the heart a honky tonk: funny and sexy and sad. The monumental "Stand By Your Man," her signature song, rages against her will and was used against her by the religious right as well as by inelegant readers and mainstream critics. The fourteen singles she recorded with Jones—called love songs, but mostly heartbreak songs—form an explicit canon that argues in favor of heterosexual marriage despite obvious traumas. Her last big country single, "Womanhood," much like Tom T. Hall's "Margie's at the Lincoln Park Inn," argues in favor of adultery, but in this case with a strange subtext of piety and failure. The delicate, interwoven harmonies in the trio album she did with Dolly Parton and Loretta Lynn reflect the possibilities created by decades of friendship. All of this is partly why Tammy Wynette matters: she reflects the domestic and social politics of women in America after World War II.

My focus isn't strictly on gender, though. I argue that Wynette crafted a persona, and resisted that persona, and that this kind of persona-crafting is difficult work, work we should recognize. Unlike Michael Jackson's growing up a poor kid from Gary, or Elvis's image as a poor kid from Tupelo, Wynette's making her own identity is rarely considered. The creation of a persona is another kind of mythmaking, another way of art making, another way of being serious. She could be urbane, but hers was a persona that moved from rural Mississippi through Birmingham to Nashville, and her hardworking rural authenticity was part of it. The ambition for achievement matters, as much as the crafting of the persona.

Wynette's persona was similar to those of other female twentieth-century performers, on the surface. I think that with Parton, we see her as a dumb blonde made smart. We see her as a Mae West or a Jayne Mansfield, and so by extension we see the persona, and can grasp it. But Wynette was too clever, making her persona hermetic and seamless, rooted in the domestic, so we don't think about it as a kind of art. That matters too.

There are debates about Wynette's achievements, and about how she made art, questions about how much of the writing she actually did, about how much she was under the influence of men such as Sherrill, who has writing credits for most of her work, or Jones, who worked intimately with her, and about the politics of her songs. In particular, there have been tens of thousands of words of discussion about "Stand By Your Man," which she cowrote with Sherrill, and her public discussion of its meaning—some writers opining that Wynette was dumb or naive, or that she was herself reactionary and the song was an argument against feminism. Wynette fueled the latter contention when she performed at rallies for the third-party, segregationist presidential candidate and Alabama governor George Wallace. The most famous of these was a 1972 event some called the Wallace Woodstock, which Wynette most likely organized. Ten thousand people were in attendance at this rally, held at Wynette and Jones's Old Plantation Music Park, located on their country estate.[8] The intermingling of personal and private with professional and public that marks her work with Jones often elides how difficult and abusive he was and how controlling he may have been in their artistic process. The supposedly greatest love story in country-music history often includes

Jones hitting Wynette, threatening her with a gun, and abandoning her for days at a time.[9] Even that last KLF single is a gnarled problem: is Wynette in on the joke, is she being respected, or is she being mocked?

If the music is significant, and how we read the work is a mess of contradictory moments, then the question of how much of the biography is included in that music takes its place front and center. Wynette made work about her life, but the involvement of Sherrill and other writers also means there was some distance there. She wasn't performing her own life but creating a persona that appeared real. That her real heartbreaks were polished, faceted, and carefully set testifies to a craft that has been underrepresented. Still, it seems impossible to write about Wynette without writing about her life, and it's impossible to write about her life without thinking of it as a subject of the self-same crafting.

Wynette grew up very poor and rural, near the border between Mississippi and Alabama. But her grandparents, who helped raise her, might have come into some money in Wynette's adolescence. (Parton and Lynn have both suggested that they were much poorer than Wynette.) She was said to have picked cotton in her childhood, but later there was debate over how much she picked. She talked about having been a beautician and barmaid in her twenties, but she was singing on television at the same time, and it's uncertain how much time she really spent on either of these other careers. She might have had a beautician's license her entire adult life, but she might not have. It was important to her image that her audience believe she did.[10]

A lazy critic might assume a one-to-one correlation between her songs and her unhappy life, which was an even messier and more difficult one than the melodrama of her work conveys. Such a critic might think that every time she sang she was singing about her life, that she was engaging in reportage—and rather artless reportage at that. Or, on the other hand, that she was incapable of creation herself—that she was mostly following the lead of producers like Sherrill, of the studio band, or, when she was with Jones, of her husband. This is a limited view of authorship. She had writing credits on a substantial number of her hits, but this, too, is a limited view of it. How she performed, how she sang—that was its own kind of authorship. How she crafted an autobiography to function as a kind of persona was another kind. That she melded the persona building, the songwriting, and the performing into a singular vision, transcending that one-to-one correlation—that was her accomplishment.

Wynette was a performer. That she wrote little, and that she worked with other people's voices, means that we might need to widen and deepen our understanding of authorship.

I make the case in this book that Tammy Wynette matters because of the depth of her art, the formal qualities of her singing, and her ability to make melodramatic genius out of the mess of her life. However, I also argue that crafted presentation, work that is considered silly, such as costumes or hair or home decor, is another way of making a life into art. This book is about her figuring out how to be a woman in a world that is hostile toward women, and how to make being working class, in a world that is hostile toward working-class people, a part of her persona. It's about the art of performing and presentation. The aim is not to forgive Wynette's racial politics, complacency about institutional misogyny, or poor parenting, but to allow a complex vision to emerge, to have a serious conversation about a serious artist. And we can do that only by talking about all of it: her hits and her career downturn; her marriages and her divorces; that weird kidnapping incident; her wigs and her friendships with the women who took care of them; her live shows and her funeral; and what she might have lied about in order to tell the deeper truth.

I genuinely struggled, throughout the writing of this book, with whether to lean into a single conclusion about any of the controversies of Wynette's life. Her biographers Jimmy McDonough and Tyler Mahan Coe suggest that she faked the 1978 kidnapping and staged her harassment and the vandalism of her home that happened before and right after it.[11] If I do not believe her, do I not believe the victim in general? If I trust McDonough, and his book on Wynette, *Tammy Wynette: Tragic Country Queen*, then I don't trust her. I do trust that McDonough is an excellent researcher with a strong connection to Nashville insiders, and that he would know more than most, but I think many of the men he interviewed had their own agendas, ones that were at oblique angles to Wynette's life.

Believing Wynette might mean not prioritizing McDonough's sources' offerings. The *National Enquirer*'s continual interest means the tabloid might be more reliable than the biographies.[12] Centering Wynette's problems — involving gender, sexuality, and the domestic — allows us to examine the meaning of work in these contexts, independently of concentrating so much on aspects of her life focused on by others. This means taking seriously that which is thoughtlessly devalued in our misogynist culture. I know the artist is not the work, and work that appears to be autobiographical cannot be immediately read that way, but it would be naive to assume that a life had nothing to do with the work being made by the one living it.

One of the reasons Wynette matters is the general ambivalence of her life, and how that ambivalence inspired a career that included ambitious, transparent, and haunted work, work that should be taken seriously. Admitting that one does not know, that one cannot know, or that a life is too complex to be fully understood does not preclude our attempts at knowing, nor does it lessen the potential for tremendous gains from what we may learn. Wynette still matters because of the fruitful tension of that ongoing ambivalence.

DOMESTICITY

On May 5, 1942, Virginia Wynette Pugh was born on a farm in northeastern Mississippi, near the border of Alabama, to Mildred Faye Russell and William Hollice Pugh. Her mother was a clerical worker and substitute teacher, and her father was a farmer and musician. Her father died when Wynette was nine months old, and in late 1946 her mother married another farmer, Foy Lee. Wynette was raised sometimes by her mother, sometimes by an aunt a few years younger, and sometimes by her grandparents. She commuted to a small town called Tremont, almost an hour away, to go to high school, where she was a good student and a star basketball player. But at seventeen, she dropped out to marry a man named Euple Byrd, a local construction worker. They had three children — two before she was twenty — daughters Gwen, Jackie, and Tina, one of them born with spinal meningitis.[1] She and Euple tried to make it work throughout some of the industrial cities of the Southeast, living in Tupelo and Birmingham before she eventually left him and moved to Nashville. She would go on to marry four more men, sometimes staying married for less than a couple of years — or less than a couple of months — and to have another girl, Georgette.

That is a lot of wanting to play house, and failing to play house. For Tammy Wynette, playing house, whether she wanted to or not, was at the core of her self-understanding from childhood onward. She made that life seem less chaotic when she wrote songs about it later.

An early, major statement on domesticity, "I Don't Wanna Play House,"[2] released in July 1967, begins with a small line of parlor piano, expertly delivered by the legendarily prolific Hargus "Pig" Robbins. The licks in the introduction double down on that parlor, reminding us of where the parlor is, the literal marking an abstraction of the domestic. Robbins then allows the other musicians their space, and when Jerry Kennedy's guitar hits, it emphasizes the sheer impact of Wynette's voice.

Wynette's vocal performance in the first half of the song is steely; she draws things out, preserves herself, but also adds suspense. The whole track is slow until that punchline of an ending. It has a soft/loud/soft construction, where she whispers the first verse, then pushes that soft whisper louder and louder — until she's almost belting the chorus. She quotes a child, but the child's words are too clean and too precise, as when an adult makes up a story so that a child appears cuter than they really are. This kind of construction uses domestic authority to gain social power. In less precise hands, the move could descend into total kitsch.

Wynette's ability to work with a band, to make her voice appear to be one of a number of instruments, through the tight efficiency of her mode, results in the developing emotions being because of and not despite the mechanics of the band. This whole song is tightly articulated and spare. Wynette's performance leans into the self-aware kitsch but weaponizes it, making the domestic an aesthetic and political problem; she takes the story, what she claims she overheard a child say, and repeats it in the tone of broken adult womanhood. I mean *domestic* here to have all the social and political weight that is imposed when the topic is broached, to include all the conversations about sex, gender, race, and labor that are attached to ideas of home—and, especially for Wynette, the problems of geography as well. The song never quite lands as a slice of life but instead is a well-articulated allegory, a country song about country singing. This is made especially true by the production.

"I Don't Wanna Play House" is like "Apartment #9," and perfects its themes. The metaphor of actual real estate in "Apartment #9" is taut, one story told with remarkable efficiency, riding that steel line; "I Don't Wanna Play House" widens and deepens Wynette's themes—adding the voice of a child, making an already lonely context just devastating.

The songwriters and producers Billy Sherrill and Glenn Sutton were the architects of the lush, melancholic sound (later called Countrypolitan) that Wynette would become known for. Though she doesn't have a writing credit on this song, even at this early point we hear how she sings against Sherrill and Sutton's wall-of-sound production, the almost-crying, the knothole-in-the-fence aesthetic. A classic Nashville story song, ruthless in its emotional power and bolstered by a tight studio crew, "I Don't Wanna Play House" would become the template for the rest of Wynette's work.

Sutton and Sherrill's songwriting has the same structure as a joke but moves toward the tragic: beat, beat, and then punchline, but instead of a laugh, there's a cathartic release. And the catharsis comes from the simplest, smallest moment. The narrator overhears her daughter talking to "the little boy next door" about playing a game of house. The first beat is her seeing the children playing outside; then she goes outside, moving on to actual listening, and before she tells us what exactly is being said by the children, her eyes go dim from tears and she drops her head in shame. That's the second beat. The punchline is repeated three times, functioning as both a chorus and a key change that introduces the second half of the chorus:

> I don't wanna play house,
> It makes my mommy cry,
> 'Cause when she played house
> My daddy said goodbye.

Listening to Loretta Lynn sing this song and comparing her version to Wynette's is instructive. Lynn sings it on her 1968 album *Fist City*.[3] The fact that hers was released within a year of Wynette's in itself isn't unusual; country music at this time had a quick turnaround, and it was common for singers to cover a hit song within a year of the initial recording. But Lynn maintains one tone for the entire recording — she doesn't go from quiet to loud. Wynette is faster than Lynn, but she pauses at the chorus. Wynette's ability to sing instead of speaking is a mark of emotional control; Lynn's speech singing doesn't have the same emotional impact. Wynette's talent as a singer and as an interpreter is central, even at this early stage. Still, Lynn was the only one aside from Wynette who was self-aware enough to know that she was playing kitsch, and taking that kitsch deeply seriously, to know it could be important and heartrending, and also kind of tasteless.

Other recordings of this song reject Wynette's good bad taste. Connie Francis's version appeared on the adult contemporary charts about a year after Wynette's came out. Francis's is more dynamic than Wynette's, but her voice lacks backbone, it floats in on a cloud of regret and sadness, the strings larded on, with a choir needlessly thickening the aesthetic of the song. Kitsch requires a kind of failed ambition; Francis's recording is too anodyne to qualify.

Francis was a pop singer, and her instincts and tastes consumed most popular genres and forms. She took what was popular in different genres, absorbed it, and reimagined it for a pop audience. Francis and Wynette shared the same way of working, one that relied on producers to push forward a specific, often femme aesthetic. Both of them had their songs recorded again quickly. "I Don't Wanna Play House" showed up on many albums of that era, on records that were each filled with covers, a novelty number or two, and the title track, which was in turn covered many other times, often in very quick succession. This single could be successfully played as a pop song, but Wynette's performance argues for it as distinctly country (Francis sings it as pop, Wynette as country — how one sings matters more than the instrumentation), an argument not only for genre but for a kind of genre where specific aesthetic choices were well rewarded.

"I Don't Wanna Play House" became Wynette's first solo country number-one song, staying in the top spot for three weeks in October of 1967. She had already had hits that year with "Your Good Girl's Gonna Go Bad," which was released in February and went to number three on the country chart, and her duet with David Houston, "My Elusive Dreams," which topped the country chart in

September. In 1968, her "Take Me to Your World" went to number one in March, and her success continued with the June number-one hit "D-I-V-O-R-C-E" and a Grammy Award for Best Female Country Vocal Performance for "I Don't Wanna Play House."[4] Though she would go on to be nominated for a number of other Grammys throughout her career, she would win only once more, in 1970, for "Stand By Your Man," which was inducted into the Grammy Hall of Fame in 1999.[5]

Wynette made work about people being at home, and especially about women at home, and this apparently hit home in the 1960s. She was rarely at home. When she was at home, she lived through a string of broken marriages with dangerous men. The dramatic irony of making great art about domestic roles while failing in them is central to understanding why she matters.

Country music demands that its musicians perform realness in the same capacity as actually being real. It seems revelatory that Wynette's most significant work is in the form of melodrama, a heightened form with spikes of exaggerated emotion and deep sentimentality. It tells tales of the real by rejecting realism. Melodrama isn't taken seriously by critics because emotions aren't taken seriously and because it's often viewed as a woman's medium — see soap operas, romantic comedies, and romance novels.

Wynette's best songs are dense tales of heartbreak, little morality plays that exist within the four-minute-or-less idea of the song itself. Wynette crafted the stories she told about her personal life by using the domestic lives she led as fodder for the songs. She only sometimes wrote lyrics and music, and Sherrill's production was as important to the success of the songs as the lyrics and music themselves.

But for Wynette, the writing occurred in the interpreting of the song—the formal choices she made in phrasing, which words to clip, which lines to extend. For example, in the first verses of "Stand By Your Man," before the chorus, where she almost speaks, and she speaks with hesitancy, the song is filled with gaps between words. Then the pedal steel warms up and the chorus rises in vocal power, and by the second line in the chorus, it has moved from ambivalence to polemic. She uses that whisper effectively in other songs, too. "I Don't Wanna Play House" follows a similar pattern, where she becomes almost brassy when the word *teardrops* enters in the chorus. This emphasis in her singing on elucidating heartbreak can also sell a weak song: her performance of "My Elusive Dreams," full of bathos, extended consequences, and a silly, overwrought narrative, breaks my heart because of her commitment.

The previous examples of Wynette's craft are all records. However, her performances also included concert appearances, television and radio performances, and interviews, as well as how she showed up in the newspapers and in her fan-club newsletters, and even how she dressed and wore her hair. She also crafted a very specific set of personal anecdotes that were traded by every journalist, every writer, and every family memoirist writing about her.

Autobiography always flirts at the edges of Wynette's music, so it doesn't seem unfair to suggest that looking at "I Don't Wanna Play House" might be a way to discuss what she wanted. To put it another way, she wanted to play house, and failed at playing house, and then didn't want to play house, and failed by not wanting to play house. The song can be used as a lens to discuss the complex and itinerant way that Wynette lived her life.

Wynette's father played live at house dances, barn dances, and the like, but he most likely didn't record. It was known that the house was full of instruments, and that Wynette was playing them from an early age. As an adult, she toured almost constantly. In lean years, or between albums, her touring provided most of the income for the household. I wonder if succeeding as a country musician, recording, and touring, was, for her, succeeding at the life her father didn't have a chance at.

Wynette was mostly a honky-tonk singer (she sang hard, with a twang, against the rollicking background of pedal steel, and she didn't hide her working-class roots), but a honky-tonk singer without honky tonks. She learned the genre while singing away from home, but there's something about her sentimentality, and her earnestness, that seems born from the loss of her father. That most of her work was about the failures of the domestic, about wanting and not wanting to play house, must have originated at least partially in this initiating absence.

In the year Tammy was born, 1942, the most stable job off the farm was 121 miles away, in Memphis, where her mother went to work at a defense plant for a time. That work was exceedingly common for women in those war years. In an article written for *Tennessee Historical Quarterly*, Patricia Brake Howard mentions the number of people who poured into the city to build bombs and other military supplies: by 1944, there were more than 180,000 defense workers in Memphis.[6] Men were off fighting the war, so a large portion of the workers who moved from the home to these defense plants were women. The city was also a center for jobs in government and academia, about 30 percent white-collar. There must have been a certain amount of culture shock for Mildred, moving there from the border of Alabama, with its largely blue-collar milieu.

The question of exactly how rustic Wynette's childhood home life was, especially on the farm with Mildred's second husband, is a difficult one to answer. Wynette spent most of her adulthood mythologizing her early years, and her desire for persona building over verisimilitude is well established. This is another ambiguity around playing house in Wynette's life: we don't know how much material comfort was on hand in her childhood home or how much she had to work as a child. Tremont was a small town, but not as poor as the rest of Mississippi; the high school there was new. Tammy spent time in town and made as much of a life there as she had on the farm.

In his biography of Wynette, *Tammy Wynette: Tragic Country Queen*, Jimmy McDonough notes that she was less poor than her neighbors. He quotes one of them, Agnes Wilson: "If we had a dime or a quarter pocket change we was doin' real good. Maybe Wynette would have a dollar and change in her pocket. She had money at school that the other kids didn't have. Well, Wynette was rich as far as we were concerned." There was also a story told about how Chester, her grandfather, would give her anything she wanted, including an envelope with fifty dollars in cash at Christmas.[7] If so, it was a decidedly impersonal gift, and also one at odds with the stories of poverty and lack she would tell at a later date.

McDonough continues his discussion of her childhood with speculation on exactly how much cotton Wynette might have picked. Wynette's former sister-in-law, Nancy Byrd, put some of the labor in context, claiming that "by no standards did she have to stay out of school like some of the kids did to help gather the crops," and that cotton picking wasn't necessary. McDonough compounds Byrd's testimony with evidence from a friend of Wynette's, Holly Ford: "If Wynette picked cotton, it wasn't like hard labor, that they were starvin' to death. She probably picked cotton so she could put on shorts and get a sun tan." Another neighbor said that she picked not out of economic despair but because it was expected of her by her grandfather. But McDonough quotes an ex of Wynette's who says she worked like a hand and was paid like a hand, that she not only picked cotton and was paid two dollars a pound but also pulled corn and made molasses.[8]

Playing house, then, is a kind of mythmaking and a kind of performance: performance, here, meaning the sound she made on the records, of course—the twang she never got rid of, how she moved from speaking to singing, how often she had to build up to belting. Performing was also how she interpreted those works on stage, with the rhinestone-encrusted costumes, the well-thought-out blonde wig, how she nodded along when singing "I Don't Wanna Play House"—a subtle motion intended for the cameras and one she perfected in the early 1970s and continued until the late 1980s. Look, also, at how she told the same anecdotes to journalists—the one about how she picked cotton, or the one about how she always kept her beautician's license, or the one about how no one understood her version of "Stand By Your Man." See how she played at being a housewife—there are stories about her inviting guests to her house for ham and dumplings. Or how, when she was married to George Jones, they built a music park in the backyard of their home, and everyone visited.[9]

How Tammy sang and how Tammy lived were indistinct, crafted personas, and their own art making.

There are two stories that seem relevant here that people in Wynette's circle have spoken and written about. The first is that Wynette often said that she chose to work in the house as a child instead of picking cotton, but she also sometimes said that she picked cotton.[10] Wherever she was, whatever rhetorical point she was trying to make, she told the story that was convenient to the message she wanted to deliver. Wynette had a vexed relationship to the domestic, so her deciding to rhetorically move from one space to another underlined the ambivalence she felt about (any) home life. She didn't want to be the kind of person who played house unless it made her more commercially viable. She was very good about sliding out of one kind of southern myth into another kind of southern myth in order to perform authenticity—something that both home work and picking cotton can speak to.

Tyler Mahan Coe tells another story, repeated by other people around Wynette, that one day she wanted to go to the county fair and her grandfather said she had to finish the day's work before she could go. The day's work was picking a certain amount of cotton in a gunnysack and then putting it in a machine for sorting—an amount here defined by weight. Instead of picking the weight in cotton, Wynette put rocks in the bag—a fact that wasn't discovered until she was well on her way to the fair.[11]

This story has a number of things going on. It shows that Wynette could be arrogant, that she didn't think she had to do the same kind of work as other people, and that she chose the city lights over rural labor. Also, rocks in the sack were dangerous, they could get spit out and genuinely hurt someone. And finally, she was getting paid for not doing the work she was called to do. But there is a rascally charm in the story of rejecting labor in pursuit of other excitements and refusing to suffer boredom.

When Wynette says through the voice of a child that she doesn't want to play house, I think of her as Roy Clark, singing his 1970 hit "I Never Picked Cotton":

> I never picked cotton
> But my mother did, and my brother did
> And my sister did, and my daddy died young
> Workin' in the coal mine.[12]

Like wanting to play house and not wanting to play house, Wynette wanted to be known as someone who picked cotton and also someone who escaped from picking cotton.

Wynette kept a Lalique bowl full of cotton buds in her home in Nashville. When people mention that home-decor choice, they concentrate on the cotton but ignore the Lalique. The cleaned and processed agricultural artifact in a bowl marked her arriviste taste — that's Wynette's negotiation between class and taste, between wanting and not wanting, and it's almost too perfect a metaphor.[13]

HIGH FEMME ARMOR

After Euple Byrd moved Wynette to the small town of Red Bay, Alabama, she started beauty school; for economic reasons, they moved to Tupelo, Mississippi, and then, after moving again, she did the final licensing in Birmingham, around 1963. Her mother paid the tuition. Wynette did hair for a little bit. She had escaped the farm she grew up on to go to high school in Tremont, and a few years later took a similar step up to Birmingham. Money was funneled from farms to small towns, and from small towns to big cities, as was ambition.

There was something ambitious and new about Wynette. Though country music has always claimed to be timeless, the tradition must always be renewing itself. Tradition, be it in gender norms or family rituals or musical genres, defines itself against what is new. One can't know what is new without knowing what is old, and one can't seek a return to the old ways without understanding what is new. Though a hairdressing career was a common way for women to leave the farm, choosing to do hair instead of farming, as generations of her family had done, was the first step in Wynette's balancing of the cosmopolitan and the country.

One learned hairdressing as an aesthetic exercise but

also because it was a job that was relatively easy to get and one that paid well, depending on the clients and the location. Though, in her autobiography, written with Joan Dew, Wynette makes clear that the idea that it paid well for the time and place might not mean that it paid well enough to raise children on, when she had little assistance from her husband: "I was making only $45 per week at the beauty shop, trying to support myself and my children on that, and living in a $23/month government housing project apartment with bare concrete floors."[1] (She would use this apartment as inspiration for her heartbreak masterpiece, "Apartment #9.") Unlike the blue-collar jobs commonly done by men, hairdressing was done in communities of women, so at least a worker could set her own hours and find her own clients. This was paramount in families where both spouses were working and there were children in the mix.

Other things also held Wynette's attention during the couple's year and a bit in Birmingham. One of her side gigs was working as a barmaid, which frustrated Byrd since he thought it was no place for a lady, and it made the possibility of stepping out more likely. She also started singing seriously for the first time. There is less written about this than there is about her work as a beautician, but there were stories about her singing at a bar (though Wynette doesn't name the bar in her autobiography, nor is the name mentioned in McDonough's biography).[2] It's never been determined whether that singing happened while she was waiting on tables or on some kind of stage.

Although her other early adult jobs aren't discussed in much detail by her or others, the lore of the beautician's license followed Wynette throughout her career as a sort of origin story, and there is a poignant moment near the end of her autobiography where she talks about how her life and her children's were better because she didn't remain a hairdresser: "And I think it's lucky that my work happens to be music, because otherwise I'd still be a hairdresser, working long hours every day, coming home at night after being on my feet steadily, too tired to have fun with my kids and too poor to buy them nice things or take them to exciting places."[3] There is class recognition here: she knew she wouldn't have had financial success in life if she had stayed a beautician and a barmaid, but without having done that work she wouldn't have had the material, the understanding, or the ability to show solidarity with an audience that pretended to be, or at one point was, working class.

There are different kinds of working class that Wynette could have emphasized in crafting her persona. For example, she didn't really talk about being a barmaid. She could have said that she was working at a bar for a while, that she discovered she liked singing, and that someone found her at a honky tonk. It wouldn't have been any less accurate as a story, but the spin would have shifted how we view her music. To become famous is to craft a life history out of the nuances and complications that exist, and to prioritize one intervention, choosing one path over the others. For Wynette, the one path was that license.

For decades, Wynette claimed that she maintained her beautician's license. She mentions having the license or working as a beautician more than thirty times in her autobiography — telling stories about visiting her daughter in the hospital while still in her beautician's whites or not having enough money despite the labor she did.[4] In interviews, in most profiles, in the biographies, and in her friends' reminiscences, the centrality of this cosmetologist's license is repeated again and again. It even comes up in her website bio: "Never believing her own hype, Tammy kept her beautician's license up to date noting 'she could always go back to hairdressing.'"[5] Samantha Drake discusses it in a 2017 *Country Living* article.[6] Miles Corwin drops it into a profile in the *Los Angeles Times* announcing Wynette's death in 1998.[7] In a *South Florida Sun Sentinel* story dated a decade before that, it's mentioned by Jim Presnell.[8] McDonough's biography quotes Emmylou Harris noting it.[9] The only possible exception is daughter Georgette Jones, who, in her memoir, adds a little doubt: "It's true that she kept her beautician's license current, or at least she renewed it most years."[10]

Even Dolly Parton has told stories about Wynette's beautician's license. In a profile for the *New Yorker*, done in 2009 to promote the Broadway adaptation of the movie *9 to 5*, Lauren Collins quotes Parton as saying, "Tammy Wynette, she was a beautician back home, kept her license up to date every year, even though she became one of the big stars in the whole world. . . . I used to always beg her, 'Can I have your card number so I can go buy stuff at the beauty-supply houses?'"[11]

Being a woman from mid-twentieth-century Mississippi and Alabama, where presentation and decorum were required, was central to Wynette's self-understanding, and it's a conception shared by many of the women in her life as well. There's an intense sanctity to the image of Dolly Parton coming to the hospital to wash the makeup from Wynette's face and then paint and powder it again, almost as if preparing a corpse for burial.[12] This makeup has a host of purposes: to save face, to give good face, to face the music and dance, and, in Wynette's case, to face down grief. To embody all of this requires full high femme armor.

Contending with the juxtaposition of Wynette's high femme beauty and the heartbreaking melodrama of her songs is vital for an audience's greater understanding. This could include a conversation about "Your Good Girl's Gonna Go Bad," in which, as I discuss in more detail later, the narrator adjusts her armor, going for "painted up, powdered up" to become the type of woman her husband seems to prefer or to attract other men; or her last country hit, "Womanhood," also discussed at length later, containing the phrase "step into my womanhood," which the narrator uses to steel herself for sex that God might not approve of. It can also be seen in her cover of "Satin Sheets,"[13] where she talks about how even though she's sleeping on satin, she cries, and even with a "big long Cadillac / tailor-mades upon [her] back," she wants to be set free. It's a song that recognizes that the desire for armor can be as much of a trap as it is a liberating force, in this case the armor of the luxury items and the admiration and respect they bring from others. That tension can also be seen in 1975's "I Still Believe in Fairy Tales," a tactical belief if ever there was one.

How Wynette performs gender, as a fracturing of the self, is effective because that self has an aesthetic to break from, the aesthetic at the time being partly about how serenely a woman moved and how polite she could be — especially a southern, country woman. She didn't break from it, she held to it, and for her perhaps that was more damaging. Wynette was always serious, and sometimes severe, in her public presentation. Even at her most melodramatic, she moved only subtly on stage, often standing still. She was polite to people who interviewed her, nodding and smiling slightly when people asked her questions about what she was wearing instead of about what she was singing, especially in early appearances. On *The Bill Anderson Show* in 1967, Anderson tells her, "This new one is gonna be probably the monster of them all" (the new one being "I Don't Wanna Play House"), and she responds, "It's doing fine, I'm real proud of it."[14] Part of this is feminine modesty, but it's also Wynette knowing exactly what she has in front of her and being able to claim it without excess. On *The Wilburn Brothers Show* in 1969, she sings "Stand By Your Man" on a porch in a stage set — she sings the entire song, even the belted portion at the end, sitting down. (Nearly thirty years later, in a May 1997 performance at the Grand Ole Opry, she tells the audience as she prepares to sing the same song, "I always sit on this song, I don't know why.") She's wearing a butter-yellow suit and that ever-present bouffant, and her voice has significant volume, so much that she doesn't have to stalk the stage.[15]

Her femme presentation was very different from Parton's, with Parton's sense of humor and bawdiness. Parton tells talk-show hosts she dressed like the "town tramp" in order to get out of her small Tennessee town.[16] Parton's femme choices are entirely about her ambition. Wynette joked and played along in the creation of her own image, but the joking and play were attached to domestic choices that made Wynette appear less autonomous. Think of how she looks into George Jones's eyes in live performances they did together in the mid-1970s, regardless of how difficult they were to each other the night before and regardless of how sad the song is: as they look into each other's eyes, she's more animated than in her solo performances and she works with Jones, matching his stage presentation. They're making an argument for their own marriage, and for marriage in general, just as Wynette is making an argument in favor of her role as a wife and mother. The stakes are high—they're worth the sadness and heartbreak because they're so high.

The hardness of her life, the hardness of her aesthetic, and the break between person and persona made any creation—the blonde hair, the elaborate face—a kind of labor rarely alleviated by pleasure or fun. It's hard to forget your raising when you're still in the middle of it, and it's easy to make your raising totemic or iconic, or even a little bit performative, when it's well behind you.

Wynette's beautician's license was like Willie Nelson's story about growing up in Texas farm country or Johnny Cash's night in jail—it was a note of authenticity, of realness. When asked about the license, she claimed she held onto it out of economic anxiety, that she kept it in case the country music career didn't work out. But she performed professionally for far longer than she ever cut or styled hair. This is not to say she didn't keep the license, or that she didn't carry it throughout her life. Like everything about Wynette's life, the truth is more complicated. The intimacy of doing hair and making relationships is key to understanding her in every stage of her life. Her learning how to do hair and then actually doing it became a set of stories. There's a great one about Jones and Wynette getting drunk one night at their home in Franklin, near Nashville. For some unrecorded reason, Wynette decided to give Jones a new look and got out the home permanent set. Jones's home perm resembled a French poodle's coat.[17]

It's a jokey story, but it also suggests that Wynette found ways to control people via her craft, that in this moment she controlled the image of a vain man. Jones's letting her get close enough to do that is a mark of intimacy, and the politics of control is a measure of that intimacy.

This might be one of the few times Wynette actually did hair. She didn't even do her own hair very often. Wynette's persona was of a woman who appears simultaneously working class and above her roots (no pun intended). And though the myth of the beautician's license might have been central to her public persona, she hired women to do her hair and to dress her — every queen must have her courtiers. These women were important figures, perhaps the central ones in her life, and definitely the most consistent ones. Through decades of bad marriages with unstable men, her hairdressers and stylists were women she could rely on: Nanette England and Jan Smith, both of whom had extensive history with hairdressing, makeup, and costume, plus her close friend Jan Howard, who was one of the few people in Wynette's life who understood the femme armor and who talked to her about clothes, hair, and relationships but also gave her practical advice on music and her career. Howard's own recording career was substantial — seventeen albums in a little over twelve years — and she had four husbands, some of whom she performed with. She also had a complex relationship to sentimentality as a formalist construction that was similar to Wynette's.

Through her many years on the road, Wynette had a staff who took care of all of the gowns, all of the wigs, her emotional needs, and her physical needs — both on the great looping tours of America and in her life at home in

Nashville. Erin Duvall, in an article about her book *Country Music Hair*, is quoted as saying that Wynette always used wigs and that the wigs were extremely important to her. Duvall says she talked to Wynette's hairstylist on tour, England, who told a story about the tour bus catching on fire; she noted that England "flipped out" and said, "Save the wigs," before diving under the bus to get them, presumably from the luggage compartment. Duvall also talks about how the performers used wigs because they gave them a variety of looks and because hairstyling took so much time, ending with a discussion of how Barbara Mandrell started her career playing steel guitar for Patsy Cline but also did Cline's hair every night, which Cline hated because it took hours.[18]

In the space of a paragraph, there is so much in this pileup of anecdotes — there is the amazing possibility of someone dying or at least injuring herself to save Wynette's wigs and discussion of how valuable the wigs were in the daily labor of performing. With Parton, the surreal, over-the-top, camp quality of the wigs would have been obvious because her life was that artifice, that playing. Wynette, though, was playing a game where the slippage between what was artificial and what was real was more vexed, so it took more work to make people believe the wigs were real. Still, these nice people paid their money and they deserved a show.

Wynette's presentation, her high femme armor, was immediately identifiable to her audience but also to more middlebrow consumers. One of the few middlebrow publications to write about Wynette was the *New Yorker*, in a Talk of the Town piece in 1973.[19] In the piece, the writer George Trow meets Wynette and Jones in a private room on the second floor of an Italian restaurant on the West Side. Jan Smith is also there, identified only by the word *companion*. Wynette talks a little about Nashville, about what country music means, and the writer extrapolates. He talks about how sophisticates love Wynette, but they don't show for her openers. He talks about how Wynette never lost her country edge, how her songs are "slick and melodic" in a way that makes them accessible to a wider audience. He talks about Wynette's clothes, and jewels, a gold knit dress, rings on her fingers, and later, a white dress spangled with stars, about how "she looked in a way regal, and in a way country." The hair he mentions only once, as blonde and flowing around her head. The hair goes with the outfit, and the lack of detail about the hair means the writer didn't get what was happening. That he noted Jan was at dinner with George and Tammy, suggesting an intimacy among them, but didn't know exactly why she was there, marks how little popular-music critics understood the aesthetics and the affect of country hair, and how significant her hair was to Wynette.

For most of her last years, Wynette was very sick — she spent too much time on the stage, suffered broken bones, and underwent a serious of difficult surgeries, including a hip replacement. The surgeries led to infections, and to a precipitous decline. The decline was worsened by Wynette's prodigious drinking and by her pill consumption. Throughout this decline, Smith took care of Wynette — not only taking her to doctors' appointments but also advocating for her, helping her get as healthy as possible. Smith was with Wynette often in the days and weeks before she died.

It's a sentimental idea, how Wynette's first break from the farm was learning to do hair in small-town Alabama,

and how doing hair was connected to all kinds of labor—
raising babies, singing songs, and pouring beer. They were
all tied up together for Wynette, and when she wanted to
have someone near her that she trusted amid the wreckage
caused by the men in her life, she would choose her closest and oldest friends, the women she labored with, the
ones who did her hair. On this topic, McDonough quotes
Smith when he needs information from her, but he doesn't
contextualize her life or spend time on her relationship
with Wynette. It's another example of the great man theory of history, that, even in the midst of a biography of
Tammy Wynette, the vast majority of the stories we get
are about the husbands, the band members, the producers,
as opposed to the women in her life who supported and
cared for her: the material culture of female performers is
still thought to be frivolous, not worthy of serious attention, and so these women are shunted away.

In our culture, where most of the myths are written by
cis men, the stories we do have of women together have
often been of the convent, or the nursery, or the brothel,
or the harem—endless variations on the Madonna or the
whore. A similar kind of limited thinking about the roles
of women apparently applies here, as writers are more
likely to discuss how Wynette failed as a mother or a wife
than to think of her as a performer, and they're more likely
to—certain to—credit the men around her with making her successful than the women. But the women who
gathered around Wynette, both in a domestic space and
in a professional space, were the ones who together made
Virginia Wynette Pugh into Tammy Wynette. The beautician's license was an actual object, but it was also a totem,
a ticket into the world of working-class women making

meaning, a symbol of liberating themselves from a hostile place. These women were considered her support staff, but she surely considered herself one of them, and she must have valued that membership. Though attempts at social mobility for working-class people, especially women, rarely succeeded in the post–World War II period, there was more economic stability then for all kinds of workers, even musicians, even women. Along with that kind of opportunity came a measure of freedom, but women were still restricted in many ways, so they drew support and power from other women. So little was recorded about what was spoken about by these women, what was considered. And when it was recorded and distributed in the writing of men, it was dismissed as women's gossip.

How Wynette looked on the stage was as important as how she sang on the stage; it was all part of the same package. She obviously knew this, and it's fascinating that she also sang about the power that makeup and hair could have, showing her thinking about how important the public persona was as armor but also as weapon. Listening to her work, such as the hit "Your Good Girl's Gonna Go Bad,"[20] is so instructive. That propulsive steel guitar, and her twanged-out, low-slung vocals . . . she knows the difference between a good girl and a bad girl. And she knows the difference is nonsense. But it's nonsense that smooths things over, that makes life easier, as labels do for the ones using them. The performance has significant social capital and solid political heft.

Wynette worked in honky tonks and bars, and thus *had* "seen the inside of a bar room" and listened to a jukebox, as the lyrics of "Your Good Girl's Gonna Go Bad" say the narrator has not. The song's pedal steel is native to both environments. The opening is a concession, and maybe a bit of a come-on. When the chorus talks about how she's going to dress up fancy, how she's going to paint and powder herself up, that she's going to be the "swingin'est swinger you've ever had," she shows she knows how powerful feminine performance can be. There could be a reading here about doing all this work for men, but I think it's for Wynette's pleasure too, a kind of mutual seeking of pleasure. It's one of the brightest songs in Wynette's discography, one that marks a fluid gender performance, where she can move from being a housewife to a swinger, from someone who obeys domestic goals to someone who purposefully destroys them, not as a desperate pantomime but as an expression of a certain kind of joy.

The song has a more complex, sexual subtext than it appears to on the surface. When the narrator says she's going to paint herself up — is she doing so to please her husband or to make him jealous? When she makes her home into a honky tonk, that implies she will bring strange men into the house, she will be crafting her face for an audience outside her marriage. The way she sings the phrase "swingin'est swinger" suggests multiple partners. It opens the door for other possibilities, erotic ones, but also ones where the tight narrative of family is disrupted by feminine performance. Here, the autonomous choices made by women work against the expectations of the patriarchy. Wynette's personal and professional life were made complex not only by her gender but by how she performed gender, how she worked it, both on stage and in her personal life. Her social circle, made up mostly of women, helped to smooth this complexity.

SOFT POLITICS

The story of "Stand By Your Man"[1] begins during a late-night session on August 28, 1968, in Nashville. Wynette was there with producer Billy Sherrill, and the guys in the band were Bob Moore on bass, Buddy Harman on drums, Ray Edenton on guitar, Pete Drake on steel, and Pig Robbins on piano. Jerry Kennedy was out of town that night, but in the studio two days later he came up with the opening riff for Sherrill, who dubbed it in.[2] There was a delay in the session — maybe a song wasn't working, or maybe they realized they had more tape left than they thought. The band took a break, probably playing cards while Wynette and Sherrill went upstairs to his office. In the break, the two wrote "Stand By Your Man." Wynette said later, as her friend and publicist Evelyn Shriver recalled, that "a song that took [her] 20 minutes to write, [she] spent 20 or 30 years defending."[3]

The time it took to write "Stand By Your Man" has been mentioned in biographies of Wynette, in press coverage, and in the essay about the song written for the Library of Congress.[4] The story is so good that Wynette wanted it to be true, and the journalist Joan Dew didn't add any doubt about it in her discussion of it in Wynette's autobiography.[5] It wasn't until much later that Sherrill tried to complicate a narrative that was already legend. It might have been embroidered, but what about Wynette wasn't? In interviews for a 2000 NPR story and a 2013 *Wall Street Journal* article, Sherrill gives some details about the session. He says he had a piece of paper with the chords and the lyrics for a song called "'I'll Stand By You" written on it and then he changed it so it was about a woman advising another woman. When they went upstairs on a break from the studio, Wynette and Sherrill revised the song further on the spot. Sherrill says he asked her, "Do you want to hear it again?" and she said, "No, why don't we go downstairs and record this thing?"[6]

Receiving a writing credit on a song in a Nashville studio can mean someone added a few words, wrote exactly half of a song, or was given a writing credit simply because of their fame. Country music authorship has a bit of a collective quality, where being the first singer to have a hit with a song also counts as a kind of authorship. Wynette's performing skills, the way she took control in the studio, and her understanding of the factory speed of Nashville recording sessions all suggest that she deserves at least half the credit for the creation of that song. Sherrill says in the *Wall Street Journal* story that Wynette "changed a few lines," which might mean she cowrote it both in the conventional pen-on-paper sense and in the Nashville sense of crediting successful performances or personas as a kind of writing. As with much in Wynette's life, it's a thicket of both/and.

It's conceivable that "Stand By Your Man" could have been written in twenty minutes, considering the experience of its principals, and it sounds like the song was recorded about that fast too. This was Wynette's fifth album and she was touring relentlessly at that time, and Sherrill had been producing and cowriting dozens of albums, working six days a week, often late into the night. The session musicians had extensive experience even at this early point in their long careers and were capable of producing work at a monumental clip. By the end of his life, Moore had performed in the recording of thousands of songs, including songs in the 1950s and 1960s by Elvis, Bob Dylan, Andy Williams, and most of the Patsy Cline records for Decca. Harman played on many thousands also, including "Oh, Pretty Woman," "Coal Miner's Daughter," and "Ring of Fire." Edenton worked on Webb Pierce's "There Stands the Glass" (chopped and screwed a couple of years ago by Sam Hunt), Roger Miller's "King of the Road," and hundreds of others. Drake, who brought the pedal steel guitar into pop music, worked with much of the new Nashville crowd (the influx of musicians and writers from across the United States and Europe in the late 1960s and 1970s), including Ringo Starr on *Beaucoups of Blues* and Bob Dylan on *Nashville Skyline*. Robbins worked in Nashville consistently for more than fifty years, playing on everything from Bob Dylan's *Blonde on Blonde* (1966) to Miranda Lambert's *The Weight of These Wings* (2016) and beyond. Kennedy is an accomplished guitarist and former producer in Nashville and is known for his distinctive Dobro licks; his work graces songs by stars from Roy Orbison to Elvis Presley to Bob Dylan, among hundreds of other performers.

"Stand By Your Man" is a recording that says what it means. On the surface, it's an argument that, despite everything a man does to wrong a woman, her loyalty should rest in him, and in the state of marriage. But it has led to rifts, confusion, and a wide variety of readings. A review of the song's political weight, written for *Newsweek* by Eleanor Clift, made the East Coast's position clear: "Tammy [Wynette]'s music faithfully follows the notion that country music is poor folk's psychiatry . . . a salve for the beleaguered housewife who grits her teeth as destiny dumps its slops on her head."[7] It's significant that Clift is a political reporter out of DC and that she sees the song not as a song but as a political text—one that would typically be outside the traditions or constructions of country music, but this was the late 1960s and everything was political. Sherrill notes in interviews that Epic Records put a full-page ad for the song in *Billboard* magazine with just the text "Tammy Wynette's Answer to Women's Lib" and the name of the song.[8] Controversy sells records, and even though the song was more a story song than a conservative screed, that didn't mean it couldn't become one for commercial convenience. Despite what Wynette would have seen as Clift's misreading, another deliberate message against women's lib was used to sell her follow-up album. In an August 1970 issue of *Billboard*, a full-page ad trumpets, "With apologies to the Women's Liberation movement, we present Tammy Wynette's next number 1 single, 'Run, Woman, Run.'"[9]

This reading that women should put up with men's disloyalty might exist because of an effort (even by the record company) to place complexity on what is a plain song, a song without any irony or gap between what is sung and how it's sung. It's an earnest song. That said, part of why this song is a standard is that Wynette had such ability as an interpreter. Marriage, in this song, can be fairly thought to be both a kind of imposed servility and a hard-won and beautiful state chosen by an individual woman despite its difficulties. Candi Staton's version of "Stand By Your Man," in 1970, with a production that renders it a soul remake of Sherrill's dense production, emphasizes the lines about loneliness more than Wynette's does. Wynette's version is a public statement, for a public marriage, sung in a voice that takes all her lung power. Staton's version is smaller; her voice is huskier and more intimate. Resembling songs by other soul singers, it's an argument not of pain or obligation but of absence and intimacy—almost adjacent to Al Green's begging "let's stay together."

The catches and the hitches, the small gaps, and how Wynette uses her vocals in concordance with pedal steel and piano all complicate a voice that could have less nuance. Wynette's personal and artistic history is filled with the kind of domestic heartbreak that is a well for sadness. Her plainness deepens its affect, much as Hank Williams's does in "I'm So Lonesome I Could Cry," where he sings higher at the sound of that "whippoorwill."[10]

The thing about Wynette's voice is that, often, how it catches and breaks, even how it twangs, are marks of domestic melodrama in her performance. She sounds conversational against the lush sheen of the studio production. She sings as if she's trying to convince herself about marriage (especially in the last verses, where she returns to the chorus and delivers it in a way that Ethel Merman might recognize, almost like an inverse of "I Don't Wanna Play House") and, by extension, using that kind of persona to convince others. It's not only an argument about the value of marriage but almost a user guide to marriage itself. In this way, it slips between optimistic monogamy and ambivalent disbelief in its possibilities. Wynette is good at writing downers. Her most famous songs are about abandonment, lost children, and divorce. Listening to her work in context, even a song as simple as "Stand By Your Man" has a kind of abjectness to it, a desperation and sadness.

Considering Wynette in the context of her cohort, her transparency is in stark contrast to Loretta Lynn's feistiness or Dolly Parton's extremely deliberate separation of person and persona. Wynette sings plainly, conveying a simple message about the virtue of fidelity to a man while paradoxically staking her claim on independent ownership. In country music, where the owner of a song could be the writer, the first performer to make it a hit, or the performer who sings it better than anyone else, "Stand By Your Man" is one of those rare tracks where these three forms of authorship merge, deepening its legendary status.

The authorship of "Stand By Your Man" slides into what was viewed as a traditional gender performance, especially considering Wynette's relationship to producer Billy Sherrill. She plays being a woman who needs a man in this song, but that playing can also be seen in how she plays along with her producers and musicians. There were five men performing the song that night in Nashville, and there was one man cowriting and producing it. Men owned the studio in which it was being recorded and owned the labels and distribution centers that released it. The radio disc jockeys were men. Men organized the package tours and eventually the headlining tours. There was an ecosystem of men who were responsible for this song of plain moral guidance for women, and it was an open question as to how Wynette kept those men in line.

Wynette's power—as an ambitious businessperson as well as a performer who played on the difference between a persona and a person, though in a less self-aware, more ambivalent way than Parton — made the gender implications of that ecosystem even more complex. She thought the liberal critics of the song, who saw it as an example of domestic servitude, didn't understand it. In her 1979 autobiography written with Dew, which uses the song's title as its title, Wynette defends the song by discussing what is in it, as opposed to what is absent from it:

> I don't see anything in that song that implies a woman is supposed to sit home and raise babies while a man goes out and raises hell. . . . To me it means be supportive of your man; show him you love him and you're proud of him; and be willing to forgive him if he doesn't always live up to your image of what he should be.[11]

Wynette wanted the domestic, and wanting that kind of life in the midst of the second-wave feminist tumult placed her on the conservative side of the culture wars. When she's singing these songs, they're in opposition to the deconstruction of the domestic in texts such as Betty Friedan's *Feminine Mystique*. Friedan thought that "the women who 'adjust' as housewives, who grow up wanting to be 'just a wife,' are in as much danger as the millions who walked to their own death in the concentration camps," and considered the unpaid labor of the home a kind of slavery.[12] While Wynette might not have always stood by her man, she had enough marriages to know the lived reality of divorce. The song depicts a goal or even a utopian ideal more than it depicts any autobiographical truth.

"Stand By Your Man" sold well, not because of critics' reviews but because it filled a need for an audience that wasn't being listened to. The track's success was weighted with all that came with the nature of monogamy at that time, especially the domestic labor. It was a (perhaps not deliberate) rejoinder to Friedan and company. To put it more plainly, Wynette spoke for a generation of women who found value in and held onto a life that Friedan and second-wave feminists discarded. Of course, singing about this kind of labor and actually doing it are different tasks. Around the time the song was released, Wynette was capable of hiring out that work, which she did, often to women of color. Wynette even quotes a Black house-keeper, Thelma Brown, in her autobiography, using a thick dialect that is fairly close to minstrelsy.[13] What one wants, what one gets, and what one advocates that other people ought to want or get is tangled. (Also, Betty Friedan was in a decades-long monogamous marriage with a man she loved deeply.) The arguments of Friedan and her desire to emancipate women have power and legitimacy, but Wynette grew up in a sharecropping family, her father died early, and the economic stability she found in her profession was a hard-won battle often coming at the expense of her marriages. Friedan and Wynette were talking past each other, not understanding what the other was saying.

To again look at Wynette in comparison to her cohort in considering the confines (or lack of confines) in marriage, her friend Dolly Parton has been married to her (reclusive) husband for fifty-six years. We don't know about Parton's marriage.[14] She's cagey about personal details and doesn't make work about it. Loretta Lynn, whose songs of domestic tumult are funnier and less sad than Wynette's, was married to her husband for forty-eight years. Loretta and Oliver "Doolittle" Lynn fought, and Loretta, in her second memoir, said he stepped out, he spent money that wasn't his, and he hit her.[15] But they stayed together, they stood together.

These three women had in common an unrelenting work ethic, a traumatic history of rural poverty, and a belief in the South. Wynette's particular belief in the South makes "Stand By Your Man" even more complex. While the sexual politics of the song might be defensible—it's nice to think of coming home every night to a woman who loves you, to raise babies in the stability of monogamy—this narrative of babies and monogamy, considering Wynette's time and place, is heavily influenced by race and class. Think of the generations of Black and Brown women who did the domestic labor that made monogamy and child rearing a more easily achieved goal for rich white women. Wynette understood the song's political power, so when she performed it at campaign events for George Wallace in the 1970s and 1980s, the generic "man" of the husband slid cleanly into the specific "man" of the political leader.

Wallace was convinced that social integration would result in mixed marriages, and that mixed marriages would result in the collapse of the family—for him, *the family* meant specifically the white family. By performing at Wallace's events, at least the ones before he apologized for defending segregation, Wynette was giving a de facto endorsement not only of his campaign but also of his racism and desire for segregation.[16] Wallace was a candidate who violently supported segregation and sought to deny Black citizens entry into public life, and Wynette backed him in the hopes of preserving a white and heterosexual way of life as a moral necessity. Peter La Chapelle's book *I'd Fight the World: A Political History of Old-Time, Hill-billy, and Country Music* makes the argument better and with more space than I can here, but country music sought to restore and maintain order.[17] For Wynette, the order she sought to maintain was that of her family — she was concerned about how her family members were affected by her work, which was filled with an anxiety about their instability, and by her life, which was unstable. In the South, as described above with regard to Wallace, anxiety about the family was often code for anxiety about the white family. The soft power of the family provided another way of controlling discourses of race and gender. Wynette might never have said anything directly about race, but she said a lot about gender — and at the expense of a direct quote, there is a mountain of indirect evidence.

There is a feminist notion that the personal is the political, one that Wynette tried to avoid mentioning. In interviews she often dodged or evaded the larger political context of some of her choices. If she had not sung this song for Wallace's rallies, an argument could be made that the social context of Nashville at this time was sublimated, that racial issues were not explicitly present but were kept beneath the surface. However, her work on these campaigns added a chapter to the long history of white women's self-selected, politicized docility being weaponized against African Americans: it was not nearly as bad as Carolyn Bryant Donham's lying when she claimed Emmett Till whistled at her, but it was not without social violence of its own.[18] Standing by your man as a white woman — be it a husband, or George Wallace, or the history of the Confederacy, or the patriarchy — has economic and social power in the South.

There is a reading, then, in thinking about the interiority of something like "Stand By Your Man," where a politics of personal satisfaction and social steadiness can convey not an internal striving but an external political act. Part of the reason Wynette was capable of moving from the closeted politics of the domestic to the wide-open politics of gubernatorial and presidential races was how much money "Stand By Your Man" made. It was a top-twenty pop hit and went to number one on the country charts, and, more than five years later, it sold enough for a silver record on the British charts.[19] More importantly, it shifted how we understand Tammy Wynette as a performer. Before "Stand By Your Man," her singles had the kind of heartbreak melodrama that was well respected in Nashville but did not break beyond the walls of Music Row. She was considered a very good singer of some excellent songs by the cognoscenti, but "Stand By Your Man," through her skill and the skill of her band, took the melodrama of her previous work and pushed it into the national conversation. Questions about how to talk about the domestic, how to construct meaning about lives that were hidden, were very much part of the zeitgeist at that time. Wynette made a standard.

If it was popular then, and was a signature song for more than two decades, it's much less popular now. There are reasons for this: aside from one unexpected hit with the British dance band the KLF, Wynette didn't have any significant comeback singles in the last few years of her life, though with Lynn and Parton she recorded a fairly successful traditional album in the decade before she died — her last significant work. It might be less popular now because of the way that the stakes seem higher, that those on the violent far right have no patience with the gentility of Wynette (imagine Marjorie Taylor Greene quoting it); or that it can't be fully extracted from ironic readings; or that it sounds too old-fashioned to be renewed in a contemporary mode but too slick to be rescued by the neotraditional folk circle. Maybe it's too much of an iconic object to be seen as an actual text again—though people have tried. Maybe it's just that how we understand domestic labor has shifted enough that, economically, no one is standing beside anyone.

If "Stand By Your Man" is too iconic, then Lynn's songs are slightly more fashionable because they can be appreciated ironically. Lynn's idea of domesticity sometimes resembled more of a Tom and Jerry cartoon than a real marriage. She made great songs, work like "The Pill," or "Fist City," or "One's on the Way," but songs that were filled with jokes, and when played outside of her milieu, in bars in the Mile End of Montreal or Queen West in Toronto or Andersonville in Chicago, the joke became more about treating Lynn as an anthropological curiosity than about discussing her as an actual songwriter or performer. But being funny can take you a long way, especially if being in on the joke makes people feel superior.

Wynette's voice was sadder and less fiery than Lynn's. The domesticity that Wynette talked about was constantly under the threat of being broken, if it wasn't already smashed to pieces. Even "Stand By Your Man," one of the great country odes to fidelity, has a narrator whose voice is smaller and less assured than those of other country singers at the time. Though it plays so well across the band, it's hard to tell exactly what feelings it's broadcasting.

The team of musicians on "Stand By Your Man" is consistent, tight, and always in the pocket. The studio owners were careful about money and knew that bands that worked tightly and efficiently would save them cash. There is nothing indulgent in their playing, but there is an intense pride in their craft. This was also the case for both Wynette and pedal-steel player Pete Drake, who worked together as a consistent team, with Wynette's twang playing especially well against Drake's innovative pedal steel. Part of the innovation on this song was where that pedal steel was placed, and because Sherrill didn't want "another damn steel intro" in this one, he began it with the dubbed Kennedy guitar introduction, then brought in the steel halfway through the lines that precede the chorus.[20] In this way, the pedal steel and Wynette's voice have a mutually reinforcing twang, complicating and deepening a plain lyric. The band had worked enough with Loretta Lynn to know how to make that tight playing and that twang a joke, and how not to, and it's worth noting that they rarely tried it with Wynette (one notable exception: "[We're Not] The Jet Set," with Jones).

Allowing the listener to be in on the joke is very much Parton's strategy — but Parton is, alongside Mae West, the great American hokum artist, selling her body and her talent with a constant mix of personas. She knows that even in her saddest songs, there can be a wink or a nudge. Parton also knows how to play both ends against the middle as an artist and as a media personality. She can be modishly, draggishly queer at Studio 54 and down-home earnest singing hymns at her family church. She can talk about growing up poor but also sing work whose slick production drips with money. Parton doesn't commit to a persona, or a politics, and lets her wily, American mischief be read as an authentic self because authenticity sells records. In an interview for *Dolly Parton's America*, the 2019 podcast, Parton was asked if she thought of herself as a feminist, and she responded: "No, I do not. . . . I think of myself as a woman in business. . . . I love men. 'Cause I have a dad,

I have all those brothers, all my uncles I love, my grandpas I love. I relate to them."[21]

I am not going to quibble about Parton's definition of feminism (though I will note that it's interesting she doesn't mention her husband in the list of male family members she loves). Wynette had a much more vexed relationship to men. Though she married five of them, and her best work was about her relationships with them, even her greatest love song, her great ode to marital fidelity, is going to be a harder sell than songs of eternal love.

"Stand By Your Man" is popular with hip arrivistes in the last couple of decades because it's so earnest, and earnest songs are the easiest to ironize. There are easy ways of being ironic — such as the sped-up mall punk of Me First and the Gimme Gimmes' version of this song[22] — and complex ways of being ironic. Lyle Lovett sings a version of "Stand By Your Man" that is almost a joke and almost serious.[23] The way he sings it as a joke is sadder than Wynette's version, more resigned. Lovett's gender switch does a disservice to Wynette's voice, both her instrument and her authorship: it diminishes the fact that it's a woman singing to other women, making arguments about the nature of men.

Lovett's work shows he's just another man who loves Wynette but doesn't understand her. A new version of "Stand By Your Man" can only be simple, or done quickly, after enduring a lifetime of difficulty. Lovett's irony isn't the best way through the song, but at least it assumes the text is slippery and open to interpretation. When writers or critics write about her music, I'm not sure we can assume a strong intentional or moral lesson on top of her seemingly autobiographical expressions. Country music makes it too easy to assume that the artist is being didactic, to see personal messages from the artist to the audience. If this song is ironic, the irony rests on this gap between the iconic quality of the performance and the personal life of the performer, in the space from "it is not autobiographical" to "it is autobiographical."

There is a whole history of misogyny that Wynette sometimes self-consciously played against, where she made herself out to be just a simple singer, singing simple songs, sometimes about her life and sometimes about something more general. When someone called her on her politics, she could retreat into that kind of professionalism, and because she wasn't taken seriously, she could avoid being called out directly. We saw that with her response to second-wave feminists (who, to be fair, thought they were above working-class cultures). The battle between these factions spanned decades, culminating with the Hillary Clinton debacle of 1992.

Speaking about her marriage at a critical point in husband Bill Clinton's first presidential campaign, after rumors of an affair surfaced, Clinton put it this way: "I'm not sitting here, some little woman standing by my man like Tammy Wynette."[24] Tammy Wynette was hurt by this, and angry, after decades of being used for political capital, on either side, and not being listened to, not having autonomy. Hillary Clinton had the money and resources to leave a shitty man, and didn't — because if she stayed she kept a certain amount of power. She must have understood the concessions that allowed her to stay. She strove as Wynette did, she had anxiety about money, and she still thought she was better than Wynette, her song, and the people it represented — it was a clumsy act of self-sabotage but one that suggests Clinton thought she was better than the demographic Wynette clung to. I have some significant problems with her politics, and she could have learned a lesson from Wynette — maybe not a lesson Clinton wanted, or a lesson that conflicted with Clinton's social or political ambition. I wonder what exactly Clinton got out of her time as a lawyer and first lady of Arkansas, or her time doing political work in the South in the 1970s. What did she learn there, or did the Chicago-born striver think she was better and just want to get out of there?

"Stand By Your Man" is brilliantly sung and exceptionally performed. It sold millions of copies and lasted decades. It was important to two generations of women, whose marriages and politics were under-considered. Hillary Clinton's refusing to acknowledge the complexity of the song, hypocritically, was one example of that under-consideration. Wynette has been written about less than George Jones has, though she was equally as talented and successful. She is less visible in popular culture than Lynn or Parton, though she was as influential. She was often difficult, and prickly, and it seems significant that the more difficult an artist is, the less she is paid attention to.

Those are all spaces to make apologies for Wynette and must be considered carefully. There are more problematic reasons for taking her seriously: how white femininity functions as a fifth column for racist violence; how much potential is wasted in women's lives by bad marriages, by the idea that there is one man to stand by, and by the gap between the wealth that Wynette ended up acquiring and her working-class roots; and how that ties into the shame of poverty.

"Stand By Your Man" is enough of a porous text that it leaks and stains everything it touches, but its messiness is one of the reasons it's so important.

PAIN

There are so many kinds of pain that are key to under-standing Tammy Wynette: the originating pain of all of that absent or ambivalent parenting she experienced; the depression that might have been clinical but might have been something else entirely; the pain of failed marriages; the pain of being abused by bad husbands; the pain that comes from the anxiety of not making another hit, of lost concert revenues, of not being treated like the legend you are, of not being taken seriously at all; and the pain of the guilt that comes from considering oneself a bad mother. But there was also (perhaps plainer) physical pain caused by the heavy, rhinestone-encrusted gowns that destroyed her back and the heels that permanently mauled her feet, both worn in hundreds of shows a year for decades. This pain was the consequence of show-business labor, but Wyn-ette's physical pain didn't end with these workplace inju-ries. There was a lifetime of bad medical advice, botched surgeries, and mysterious gastrointestinal distress, and then there was a late-career addiction to pain pills.[1]

Much of Wynette's pain was made public, as a generic way of conveying women's labor. Her career was about performing a certain kind of psychic distress. But she embodied the pain of that distress. The line between

Wynette as a person and Wynette as a professional becomes very thin. A Tammy Wynette kind of pain is a kind of country singing, a genre note — it's not only the subject matter but how she sang about that subject matter. Wynette's best work ("Apartment #9," "Stand By Your Man," "D-I-V-O-R-C-E," "Womanhood") has her appearing at first tenuous, then her voice breaks, then the whole thing collapses and her voice pours forward like the water from a dam being breached. However, because that subject matter is domestic, the assumption is that her pain matched her work's pain. There are some performers for whom it's really hard to split the artist from the art. Wynette was one of those. Her psychic pain was so connected to a chaotic home life that when one listens to the best examples of a Tammy Wynette kind of pain, it becomes almost impossible to miss it. The chaotic domestic life centers her marriages.

Wynette married her first husband, Euple Byrd, young. He took her to Alabama, where she learned hair and began singing on local television. Wynette wrote in her autobiography that she was miserable with her first husband, but McDonough notes that she said in an interview she was happier in that marriage than in the subsequent ones.[2] Wynette is an unreliable narrator, but considering how miserable her marriages were, the first one could have been both the best and straight up not a good time. There were conversations between friends about the couple having profound screaming arguments, which some historians claim as mutual fights. However, Byrd was bigger than Wynette, and I think it's a reasonable possibility that he hit her. We know he had her committed. One of the pieces of "evidence" that got her committed was the fact that she took her young kids and just drove around all night. Byrd described this behavior as hysterical. She was so miserable and so sick of the fights, and of being destroyed by this man, that she asked for a divorce. She was willing to risk social opprobrium to get out of this relationship. It's easy to imagine that this young woman with three kids in a shitty marriage to a man who didn't bring anything to the table, who had no money and few job prospects, would try to find a way out, and that that might include driving until she hit on an idea or just to escape his rage.[3]

The consequence was a three-week hospital stay. We know very little about that, but we know it resulted in her receiving electroconvulsive therapy treatment for severe depression and perhaps for bipolar disorder. There is half a paragraph about it in McDonough's book and a few lines in Wynette's autobiography and in her daughter Jackie Daly's memoir, but that's all we know.[4] She certainly never sang about it. The fullest depiction of the incident was in a TV movie titled *Stand By Your Man*. Parton got a genuine movie career; Lynn got Sissy Spacek directed by Michael Apted; Wynette, at least in her lifetime, got an anonymous TV movie with a B-list actor.[5]

The movie portrayal is evidence of how unseriously Wynette's life was treated and begs the question of whether people would have taken her pain more seriously if these psychiatric treatments had been depicted not by a movie of the week but by something with more gravitas. She could have done a hell of a remix of *The Bell Jar*—with the same expectations of female complacency, the same severe depression, the same pressure until someone broke, the same crisis of desire, of men, of compulsory hetero-sexuality—in a three-minute country-pop masterpiece. She could also have told us in detail in her autobiography about the treatments and about how they helped her, or didn't. Perhaps she didn't think that episode meshed with her persona.

Wynette married her second husband, Don Chapel, after she got to Nashville. Chapel was a successful writer and producer. She was a scared new performer. He fell in love with her, because, according to McDonough, "she was pretty, she was humble, she was sweet, she was innocent." Chapel thought he owned Wynette, owned her work, and owned, if not her entire body, at least her teeth (he paid for them) and her hair (he paid for new wigs). George Jones, one of the performers Chapel wrote for, thought Chapel didn't treat Wynette well, and he wanted her for himself. He went over to their house one night and refused to leave until she moved in with him. They were soon married, and they divorced in 1975. Wynette didn't have autonomy over her life, or her body. Her work was the only thing she had power over, and this work was entwined with the men who actively sought to do her harm.[6]

Wynette tells us that Jones hit her. Jones threatened her with a gun. Jones left her alone for days at a time when they had an infant at home. Jones would scream at her in the middle of the night.[7] People seldom talk about men hitting women in country music circles, but it was common. Lynn talked about Doolittle stepping out on her in *Coal Miner's Daughter*, but we don't talk about his abuse of her.[8]

Wynette married the real estate developer Michael Tomlin next, in 1976. The courtship was only a few months, the marriage even shorter. In her autobiography, Wynette talks about needing to take a break, that she went through twelve surgeries in 1973 and for the next five years was in near constant pain.[9] But when she got a little better, she would be back on the road. To help stop this cycle, Tomlin convinced her to buy an expensive condo in a luxury building in the resort community of Jupiter, Florida, as a supposed refuge. She lived there for most of their six-week marriage, but that meant she was away from her support system in Nashville. Wynette funded Tomlin's lifestyle, as she funded this real estate venture he desired. Dew quotes her in a 1978 *Cosmopolitan* article saying that Tomlin ran up and down the beach outside of her house, discharging his weapon.[10] The marriage ended there.

Then there was her last husband, George Richey, whom she married on July 6, 1978. They had screaming fights, and he may have hit her.[11] Daly has harrowing stories in her memoir of her mother about how Richey ignored Wynette as she was dying and left her corpse lying on the couch for hours afterward, calling tabloid journalists and shady lawyers before he called the family.[12]

Wynette stayed married to Richey, according to her friends, because she was embarrassed. Shame was its own kind of pain — shame at failing at marriage, shame at being bad at men, shame at losing some of her career success and her looks. There were more sinister notions as well. In her early years with Richey, Wynette went through a series of setbacks and terrifying incidents. Their house was vandalized, it was set on fire twice, she was kidnapped (as I discuss in detail later), and she was subjected to endless harassing phone calls and threatening notes.[13] Her immediate circle thought Richey was the culprit, that she was being harassed by him, though some friends thought it was George Jones. Additionally, both Daly and her half sister Georgette Jones later said they thought there was something hinky about their mother's estate.[14]

All of this, and much of what came before it, had a deep psychic effect. Wynette's close friend Jan Smith, in her conversations with McDonough, talks about how Wynette was sad in ways that went beyond how she sang work like "Apartment #9."[15] Some of this sounds like exhaustion—not wanting to get out of bed after a tour—and some of it sounds like the consequences of choosing bad men—crying in bed after a breakup. Some of it might have been physical, and it could also have been some kind of clinical depression. That doesn't mean it wasn't possible that she was both sad clinically and sad because of her life, exhausted because she was depressed and exhausted because she worked so hard.

Wynette's pain in her work and in her life seem inseparable. Just as her sad work and her sad life were mutually constructed, a text and a persona reinforcing each other, the anxiety of the work and the anxiety of capital kept pushing her. Wynette made a lot of money, and Wynette spent a lot of money. Each of the major biographies talks about her love of shopping, and that is part of it. But she owned a music park with Jones in the 1970s that lost money, and a real estate scheme in Florida with Richey almost went belly up. Her concert revenues went down after the 1970s, and her records didn't sell as well either, and between this, the faulty investments, and not really cutting back on her lifestyle, there was serious trouble with money.[16] That this occurred at the same time that Parton was making movies like *9 to 5* and *The Best Little Whorehouse in Texas*[17] and Lynn's autobiography was being made into the very successful film *Coal Miner's Daughter*[18]—that her friends were succeeding when she was not must have caused a bit of pain.

This discussion of Wynette's psychological pain must

of course be considered in relation to her body. For the last third of her life, her physical pain was significant; after many other procedures in her adult years, in just the last decade and a half of her life Wynette went through, among other things, "an appendectomy, a hysterectomy, a gallbladder operation, four surgeries for abdominal adhesions, two bladder suspensions."[19] She also had an addiction to pain pills, though considering how many times doctors went into her body, taking pills to manage pain seems reasonable. There's a small moment in Daly's memoir where she writes about how the bodily pain caused social isolation: "A couple of days later, her stomach ache became unbearable and she was forced to see her doctor. He examined her, scheduled gallbladder surgery for the next morning and sent her straight to the hospital. She spent the night there alone."[20]

Wynette undoubtedly suffered extreme physical pain, but it was her psychological distress that seeped up through her work and rose to become almost a persona of its own. Certainly people have recognized it as a specific kind of pain worthy of being named for the country star. In the aftermath of a difficult divorce, Reba McEntire released a song in 2019 called "Tammy Wynette Kind of Pain."[21] This was late McEntire, a McEntire who was trying to figure out what it meant to have a late singing career, a McEntire who was fully in her icon stage, but an icon stage in which she wasn't selling as many albums or as many concert tickets as she had in her prime. McEntire has always been at a little bit of a distance from her songs. She sings stories, often of women, often in the midst of a domestic crisis, but the stories are told in the third person, they're smaller and more relatable than the iconic strength of Wynette at her best.

McEntire is from a middle generation, a transition

between Parton/Wynette/Lynn and the mid-1990s explosion of Faith Hill and Martina McBride. By the mid-1990s, Parton was a cross-cultural, global superstar and Lynn had become a kind of cult figure, the country singer that even hipsters could love. Wynette's reputation was a bit lost in the years preceding and the decades after her death. Though she was quickly inducted into the Country Music Hall of Fame after she died,[22] and some of her albums had been rereleased in the years leading up to her death, much of this seemed pro forma. Even the German reissue firm Bear Family Records has not made a significant attempt to rescue her work, and there are none of the deluxe 180-gram vinyl records you see with other, lesser artists.

Reba was old enough to, from her experience of hearing Wynette's work in its heyday, provide a bridge between old and new Nashville with "Tammy Wynette Kind of Pain" in 2019, but even a singer who wasn't born until 1986 is well aware of the Wynette kind of pain. Kellie Pickler's 2011 "Where's Tammy Wynette?"[23] is a great, small song that poignantly calls down Wynette as a kind of house saint for broken hearts in the same metacontextual way that McEntire later does. Pickler didn't have much of a country career and landed a job as a syndicated morning-talk-show host, so she never lived up to her musical potential. But this track, a kind of feminist remake of Waylon Jennings's "Are You Sure Hank Done It This Way,"[24] allowed for a potential understanding of what Wynette's music meant. Pickler's honky-tonk guitar and belting voice reveal a historical memory. Beginning with a musical reference to the Jones song "He Stopped Loving Her Today," it then riffs through everything honky tonk desires: the unfiltered Camels, the fellow sleeping on the couch, and finally searching "that midnight radio / 'Til I find something that hurts."

These two songs are some of the rare, sustained remembrances of Wynette, but they both center on a kind of masochism, a small, domestic masochism. Wynette's feelings were bigger, her voice was bigger, and Pickler makes the whole enterprise a tiny bit of a joke, but the songs share a deeply mutual agreement: Tammy Wynette was the person you could call on to help you wallow in and, finally, to move through your pain. However, the pain is a domestic pain. It's the pain of the cheating song, the broken marriage, and the abandoned woman. It's not that Wynette didn't have a lot of that business, but it makes one wonder whether these attempts hit the nail on the head: exactly what *would* a Tammy Wynette kind of pain be? Wynette's difficult life was full of pain, some of which made it into her art and some of which she hid from everyone but her closest circle.

Individually, all of Wynette's different kinds of pain are not uncommon. Health problems are not unusual. Domestic violence is common among country musicians, and the list of both perpetrators and victims is long: from Spade Cooley murdering his wife in 1961;[25] to the suspicious death of Shawn Stephens Lewis, Jerry Lee Lewis's fifth wife, in 1973;[26] to the "volatile" relationship of Sammy Kershaw and Lorrie Morgan in the aughts;[27] to Chris Cagle's arrest for domestic violence in 2008.[28] Pill addiction is common as well. It killed Hank Williams,[29] hastened the death of Elvis Presley,[30] put Waylon Jennings in the hospital (though that might have been the cocaine),[31] and resulted in the Icarus-like fall of Mindy McCready.[32] Same with the money problems and the career dive. But there are few artists whose style has matched their lives as tidily as Wynette's, whose life was such an efficient machine to power the work. There's something about her pain that works for people.

Tammy Wynette's pain matters because of the usual empathetic ways of being human, but it also matters because it led her to create some great work and because that great work's complexity is lost on a misogynistic Nashville. But Wynette knew that high femme has power, and she used it as a decimating weapon. Our studying that matters. It's easy to think of her as a victim. It's harder to see the stab-and-parry elegance of her best femme performances and to realize that, in her time and place, pain had an elegance.

Wynette's aestheticizing of pain seems to show that she felt it more deeply and perhaps in a way unlike anyone else, so it makes some of her choices difficult to understand and impossible to forgive, especially the men she married and how long she stayed married to men who hit her, threatened her, or stole from her. Her ego was all encompassing. She worked with some truly repulsive people. She consumed everything — time, money, resources. Her capacity for pills and booze was legendary.

Wynette chose bad men, and though one should never blame the victim of domestic violence, the choices perpetuated themselves enough that there is a frustration there. Reading about Wynette, her interlocutors ask, "Seriously, this too?" Though it may be a bad critical practice, there is so little space between her work and her life that writing about both is irresistible, and feeds back into that all-consuming appetite. To take Wynette seriously is to take her gender seriously, the cultural and social contexts of her gender in her time and how those contexts could result in such a complex legacy. Men are allowed to engage in legendarily bad behaviors, and men in country music almost seem encouraged to engage in them; women's behaviors are policed, tightened, made smaller and more domestic. Analogously, the work of Jones and Wynette seems to have been affected by these social dictates. Jones's most significant work, work prioritized by critics such as Nick Tosches in his book on country music or his infamous *Texas Monthly* profile,[33] is of the loping, free-ranging sort. Wynette's work is of a hard interiority. It's easier to forgive damage outside the home, and it's harder to realize that the sentimental myths of motherhood can be weaponized. To take seriously a life and work like Wynette's is to not make apologies, nor treat her like we treat Jones. No one is singing a song called "George Jones Kind of Pain."

MELODRAMA

On October 4, 1978, Tammy Wynette sought help at a stranger's house eighty miles from her home near Nashville. She was in a state of shock, with significant bruising on her face and body, and a broken cheekbone. The new yellow Cadillac her ex-husband George Jones had bought her was found in a ditch a few miles away.[1]

Any reckoning of Wynette's life — in her daughters' books, the biography by McDonough, or Coe's podcast — has to come to terms with this event. The more traditional reading is to have a single opinion about what happened and to provide evidence. The problem is that after reading primary sources, and work done about the kidnapping after the fact, I ended up thinking two things: First, all the possibilities (that she faked it or that Richey faked it, to distract from poor record sales or to hide domestic violence, or that it actually happened) strike me as plausible, but none of them seem to me terribly likely. The second thing is that, again, Wynette's life is rarely taken seriously; to understand this event, one has to remember that her life was filled with activities that could harm memory: drinking, taking pain pills, undergoing the electroconvulsive therapy that Byrd inflicted on her, and enduring the domestic violence of her first few husbands. To take

Wynette's story seriously is to realize that we can't know, that the ways she tells stories and remembers stories are pockmarked with corporal acts of non-knowing.

The stranger in the house where Wynette turned up, Junette Young, who was a big fan, took her into her home, and the police came to take statements, beginning what would prove to be an inconclusive investigation: they didn't succeed in arresting anyone or investigating the follow-up threats. Wynette's daughter Jackie Daly talks in her book about a jailhouse confession from someone who was locked up in Virginia when the crime took place; then she mentions the gossip following the kidnapping about what may have happened. Neither she nor another daughter, Georgette Jones, spend time talking about the possibility of a thorough police investigation in their books.[2]

Two weeks later, Wynette told the whole story to *People* magazine. She got the cover. She claimed she had traveled about thirty minutes from her home in Franklin, Tennessee, to the Green Hills mall, where she bought clothes for her daughter and took some jewelry to be repaired. When she was all done and was getting back into her car, she told *People*, "I felt a poke in my side and heard a man's voice say, 'Drive!' All I could see was a brown glove, a lot of hair on his arm and two inches of gun barrel." The man was in the back seat of the car, with pantyhose over his head. He forced Wynette to drive for twenty minutes before stopping her to tie a pair of pantyhose tightly around her neck, and then he drove for another sixty or seventy miles through the back roads of rural Tennessee. She stated that she never saw the face of the perpetrator and didn't recognize his voice.[3]

All of Nashville was talking about this event, both

before the *People* story came out and immediately afterward. Details didn't add up, motives were impugned, and everyone had a theory about what might have happened. Some people thought Wynette could actually have been kidnapped. Other people believed it was a publicity stunt designed to stir up sympathy and revive her career before the release of her new album, *Womanhood*, or to cover up an affair. Others thought it was an attempt to hide abuse by her new husband, George Richey, who had a reputation as someone who physically abused her, or an attack by former husband George Jones.[4] There was also the possibility, I think, that Tammy Wynette, with her history of mental health crises and addiction to pharmaceuticals, might not have known exactly what was going on.

In this moment the myth almost swallowed the woman, and the metatexts of scandal, desire, gossip, and marriage overtook the actual singing and performing. Wynette's life and her music were always entangled, but for a long time the music had come first. Now there was a shift.

Wynette biographers have not spent a lot of time on this incident. Jimmy McDonough's biography devotes only a few pages to it. Jackie Daly spends a little more than five page on it, and Georgette Jones spends only two.[5] No one has explored the details of the kidnapping or gone through each of the possibilities. Few have discussed the sociocultural implications of this event: what it could mean given new understandings of domestic violence, for example, or of mental illness, or of what exactly money does to people who don't grow up with it.

I don't have an argument as to what may or may not have happened. The only people who would know are Wynette and her attacker. She is dead, and he is unknown.

But I want to take the story seriously, discuss each possibility, and consider the cultural subtext that's been
missed. I think this approach is fairer to Wynette than to
try to argue for one scenario; it also illuminates the crisis
of class she embodies and the ways in which family inter-
sects with capital.

The first possible way to understand what happened
to Tammy Wynette on October 4, 1978, is to take her at
her word and accept that she was actually kidnapped and
beaten.

Wynette was a public figure known to be both wealthy
and extravagant with her spending. McDonough's biography features interviews with several of Wynette's close
associates discussing her spending, and the two memoirs
written by her children include stories of her long after-
noons shopping.[6] She was a tabloid staple and her shopping provided regular fodder, so the idea of her going
shopping at a mall, even though she was a celebrity and
probably would often have been mobbed, isn't surprising.

The Green Hills mall started as a strip mall in 1955, but a
decade later it was enclosed. Around that time, two large
department stores, Castner Knott and Cain-Sloan, opened
in the new, indoor mall. Both of these were venerable
Nashville retail establishments — with Cain-Sloan eventually becoming Dillard's. The stores were previously down-
town, and this new location out toward the suburbs was a
major shift in social and commercial power from Nashville
proper to affluent suburbs like Franklin — suburbs that
were supposed to be safer, but would prove to be ruinous
for Wynette.

Before the kidnapping, Tammy Wynette endured years
of mysterious stalking and threats. People would call

and hang up or call and repeat obscene suggestions. She noticed people she didn't know following her when she was driving. Mysterious people would visit her property, according to security guards. Her house was vandalized. Once, the words *whore* and *pig* were written in red lipstick and paint on the outside of the house; similar words were etched on glass and written on a mirror. Eight X's were once written on her back door. Another time, the entire back half of her home was set ablaze, one of several fires that broke out there. Men in Nashville often thought she was faking or staging these things. Some people thought it was Don Chapel, her second husband. Typically, for the era, it was assumed that Wynette herself was responsible — either she was faking the harassment and property damage or it was a consequence of her domestic choices.[7]

There was some police involvement, but the cases were never meaningfully investigated. The 1978 *People* magazine mentions these crimes in the same article as the kidnapping, not exactly suggesting a causal link but hinting at a connection. The statements from the police about the kidnapping were contradictory. They called it puzzling pretty immediately, but within a few days, they claimed Wynette was faking the kidnapping.[8] This might be good police work, but it could also be another example of how Wynette was just not taken seriously.

We really only know what Wynette tells us, and it's likely she held back as much as she told. Also, there's no reason to assume we're talking about calm and confident master criminals. It's possible that Wynette's kidnappers had no idea what to do with her once they had her. Think of it as something scripted by the Coen brothers — as low farce instead of high tragedy.

The second way to examine this incident is to consider it from the angle of Tammy Wynette carrying it out herself, or with help. There are strong reasons to believe that Wynette might not have been kidnapped by an attacker. In her memoir and in a later interview, Daly provides the two most believable ones, partially quoting remembered conversations with her mother and relying on other hearsay. She claims that either Wynette was faking the kidnapping by herself or that she and Richey schemed together. "Why would she have left her car, containing purchases that she purchased that day, unlocked?" Daly asks in her book. "Why would kidnappers take her away in her car, a flashy yellow Cadillac that was easily recognized, instead of their own car?" The media at the time also noted that Wynette had forty dollars in cash and almost thirty credit cards with her, but none of these were taken.[9] However, none of this takes into account the nature of Wynette's injuries. There is no note in the press or in the biographies about how someone could hit themselves with enough impact to cause a black eye or a broken cheekbone.

Daly discusses the possibility, suggested by some people in Nashville, that the kidnapping was staged in an attempt at getting better publicity.[10] Wynette's records weren't selling as well as they used to, and her style was a little out of fashion. The thinking might have been that sympathy would help with record sales.

This is an unprovable thesis. It requires access to Tammy Wynette's inner life and knowledge about how she was feeling about her sales and her career, or about going out on her own. But looking at the few years before the kidnapping, one can certainly question how well her career was going, and wonder how to jumpstart a career that seems to be dormant. Wynette's messiness rarely entered the public arena like this, and if this was a publicity stunt it was very different from television appearances or Christmas albums—her other attempts to spike sales. The kidnapping was an anomaly. One of the ways it was an anomaly was that despite the public nature of some of her confessions, Wynette could also be quite private. She didn't speak publicly about being harassed until the *People* magazine article. She didn't talk very much about her psychiatric hospitalization. She didn't mention, until much later, that George Jones threatened her with a gun.

The year 1978 was a transitional period for country music. The genre's perpetual skirmishes over what was considered traditional country and what was considered pop were returning for another round. *Traditional* is a slippery term within country music. It's as much an ideological or social distinction as a musical one, invented to suit current understandings as much as it conforms to any historical vision. In fact, *traditional* is a word that requires so much current context it's nearly ahistorical.

The split in those years was between emerging soft rock, or "smooth," performers (the new Nashville) and the so-called Outlaws,[11] who were making work that was aesthetically strategized to work outside the parameters of Music Row (though people like Willie Nelson and Kris Kristofferson wrote for Nashville for a decade before their breakouts)—or between Nashville and Austin. You can see it in the range of hits. Country at that time could mean the thick velvet of Ronnie Milsap or the rough burlap of Waylon Jennings. It was also the heyday of Barbara Mandrell, whose songs of heartbreak, such as "Sleeping Single in a Double Bed," had an ironic jauntiness, a response to domestic heartbreak being made rigorously formal, not unlike what marked Wynette at her best.

Wynette, however, lacked both the roughness of the Outlaw movement and the softness of new Nashville. This is indicated by her sales. "I'd Like to See Jesus (On the Midnight Special)," the first single released from *Woman-hood*, peaked at only number twenty-six on the *Billboard* country charts, although the second single, the title track, peaked at number three. The album itself had disappointing sales, peaking at number fourteen on the *Billboard* country album chart, after a career of significant number ones for Wynette.[12]

The singer's history with the Country Music Association Awards should also be noted. The awards took a definitive pop turn in 1978 — Crystal Gayle, Loretta Lynn's much younger sister, won for female vocalist of the year. Whereas Lynn was from Butcher Holler, Gayle was an urban sophisticate escaping small-town life, someone who had managed to get above her raising. Dolly Parton won entertainer of the year at the 1978 CMAs. Parton and Wynette were friends, having worked together for decades, so they had a lot of history, including time working with Porter Wagoner. Parton could sell out without losing the authenticity Nashville craved, but Wynette didn't really know how to change her sound, and she didn't know how to write for new audiences.

Wynette, in some ways, was damned if she did and damned if she didn't. Her lush production worked against how the Outlaw movement saw itself. The Outlaw movement was largely an aesthetic one, one that claimed not to be overproduced, to instead be raw, or real. To be raw is as much of an artificial aesthetic consideration as any other, and authenticity can be performed in an evening gown as easily as it can in biker gear; but the backlash against Wynette (and by extension her producers) was that she was too slick. On the other hand, the soft, quiet production of John Denver or Olivia Newton-John lacked the pedal steel, the twang, and the hook in the voice that Wynette had — it had a different kind of lushness in production. Wynette was too hard for the softness of one dominant mode in Nashville but too soft for the other. For the first time in her decades-long career, the queen of country music didn't fit in her own queendom. As well, the women in the Outlaw circle, although incredibly talented performers and sometimes songwriters in their own right, tended to be wives or girlfriends. In 1975, when Waylon Jennings was singing "Are You Sure Hank Done It This Way," no one was asking the same question about Kitty Wells.

Wynette worked hard, she toured relentlessly, she connected with long-time fans, and she knew how to maintain a fiercely loyal audience. She wasn't even nominated for the 1978 CMAs, which must have stung, but a lack of nominations and disappointing sales didn't prevent her from playing hundreds of gigs a year, mostly sold out — not glamorous gigs, but steady ones.

Wynette knew the way the market was going; she knew who her competition was, and she knew she no longer fit into the ecosystem. There must have been some anxiety about being outsold by other artists, and it could be that the change of taste in Nashville caused her a certain amount of panic about her ability to get back into the newspapers, to sell that new record, to get some attention and love when she was feeling ignored by a public that may have moved on.

It must also be said that Wynette was an industry unto herself. She had to deal with paying her bills, including those from the failed business ventures she had gotten into with Jones. She had to pay the usual bills performers had, for their bands, tour buses, and staff; the famous person's bills, for servants, lawyers, publicists, security, and property maintenance; plus the kinds of bills that only come when you have enough success to think that building a music park in your image is a good idea.

In a you-gotta-respect-the-hustle kind of way, it's better to think of Tammy Wynette as faking the kidnapping as a radical act of camp self-fashioning, as a fuck you to the people controlling her career, as a way of showing off her capital, as a way of wresting the narrative away from the men in her life, as a way of owning the medium, as one great cornpone piece of performance art.[13] Perhaps it was akin to Jerry Lee Lewis's setting fire to his piano, or Elvis's Jungle Room, or Webb Pierce's custom Cadillac, or any of the other weird, elaborate shit Nashville men did when they were too drunk or too loopy on pills and had no one to say no to them.

If it was a kidnapping, the reality is much worse. It's an example of the world ignoring a woman who says she's been a victim of violence, ignoring her because she's too messy or uncontained and women should be quiet and self-contained, even Wynette. The melodrama of Wynette's life, and the melodrama of her songs, make it seem like the actual consequences of the violence in her life were dismissed. The stalking, the being threatened with firearms, the being verbally or emotionally abused, and the being hit were all considered Tammy just being Tammy. This was especially true when it was her husbands doing the harm.

Each of Wynette's five husbands abused her, and the

last one, George Richey, was the least liked, by Wynette's family and by her fans. Though it was her longest-lasting marriage, there were ongoing concerns about emotional abuse and possible financial malfeasance. Richey had some money of his own before he married Wynette. He had a reputation as a yeoman songwriter from working on the epic heartbreaker "The Grand Tour," which Jones recorded,[14] and was the musical director of *Hee Haw* between 1970 and 1977; he knew the scene well enough that his assuming the role of his wife's manager is understandable. However, Wynette was much more successful than he was. Richey was an anxious kept man. His anxiety fed into her anxiety.

McDonough quotes Jones as saying "the whole affair was bullshit";[15] the gossip also suggests that it was faked and that Chapel, or Jones, or Richey, or any number of other figures, might have been involved. The gossip was given more credence when Daly, in a 2015 television interview, stated that Wynette told her that "she and Richey had gotten into an argument and that he had beat her, and they needed to find a way to cover it up."[16]

This isn't necessarily the same story Daly tells in her book, where she describes finding Wynette sitting on her driveway one night with luggage. They went for dinner at a cheap restaurant off the highway between Franklin and Nashville, and at that point Wynette admitted that she had set the whole thing up.[17]

Wynette endured a lifetime of abuse by men she married. Considering this abuse tragic, as opposed to being an example of the class and gender politics of the era, is an old-fashioned way of denying women's autonomy. There is an infamous anecdote told time and time again—in sources as diverse as Wynette's autobiography, CMT specials, the more official biographies, and the trashier corners — about one of Wynette and Jones's biggest fights culminating in Jones pulling a gun on Wynette.[18]

McDonough literally calls the fight between Wynette and Jones a "he said, she said," and suggests Wynette was exaggerating.[19] The implication is that Wynette was always exaggerating, that her stories were part of a grand, melodramatic narrative that denies any autonomy in her self-fashioning. Even if she was telling tall tales, they were well crafted. She was exaggerating for a purpose. This was its own kind of self-fashioning, a space that McDonough refuses to acknowledge as even possible.

The "she staged it" thesis is unclear and raises numerous questions. There are the ones about whether Wynette planned it or Richey planned it, and if the latter, was it in conjunction with Wynette? Could, considering the history of abuse, any of the planning, if attributed to Richey, be considered consensual? Did the plan that Wynette and/or Richey concocted include hiring incompetent people to commit this act? Wynette was seen at the mall that day; witnesses said they saw her there shopping.[20] The central question then becomes what happened between the mall and the farmhouse eighty miles away.

In interviews with the family at whose home she sought help, their stories are pretty close to Wynette's. She was confused and her body showed obvious signs of physical abuse.[21] Wynette's children seem to agree she faked it, even though it's hard to imagine her inflicting the injuries on herself.[22]

Richey may have beaten Wynette, and it may be that Wynette didn't want the world to know about the abuse.

However, Occam's razor tells us that the claim that is simplest is the likeliest to be true; staging an elaborate kidnapping doesn't seem to be the most discreet way of hiding these things. It might be an efficient distraction, though.

The last possibility is the one with the least evidence, but when thinking about integrating the threads of Wynette's life, it seems necessary to consider it. Wynette married Euple Byrd when she was seventeen and he was twenty-two. It was her first marriage and his second. Euple thought Wynette might have been stepping out on him, "stepping out" as a euphemism for adultery but also stepping out in the sense of moving past her role as wife and mother. The role of wife and mother was stressful. They had three babies in four years. The marriage went poorly. Euple was controlling. She eventually left in the dead of night, moving from Alabama to Nashville.

Euple Byrd's history of abuse with Wynette culminated in his committing her and signing off on courses of electroconvulsive therapy, as mentioned previously. "Shock therapy" was crude at that point, and doctors didn't pay close attention to the side effects. There was also a cultural history of keeping mental illness quiet. It's not something Wynette mentioned much in her lifetime, and it's often rushed past in the official biographies.[23] It must be remembered that being abused can cause depression, but depression can also be something that men label women with to control them. Men call women crazy when they leave, when they want to no longer be abused.

One of the side effects of electroconvulsive therapy is memory loss, gaps in knowing where one is or how one got there.[24] One of the side effects of opiates is a similar blacking out. If we can think of Wynette as having experienced trauma, and that doesn't strike me as outside the realm of possibility, one of the side effects of that is a kind of dissociative state. This is, again, unknowable. But if we want to talk about the full history of Wynette's life, then all of this is part of it.

The only things we know about this case are that Tammy Wynette was at a mall near Nashville in 1978 and a few hours later she was in a stranger's driveway eighty miles away. Trusting Wynette in 1978 means trusting that she was kidnapped by a man with pantyhose over his head. Trusting her more journalistic biographers means recognizing that Wynette was prone to self-creation, that Wynette in 1978 could not be trusted. Trusting Jackie Daly means believing her claims that her mother told her it was fake. Trusting scholars of trauma means acknowledging that memory can become unreliable under the effect of abuse or psychiatric interventions, especially early modes of electroconvulsive therapy. It's frustrating to think that smart people haven't connected the history of abuse with the possible kidnapping. It's even more frustrating to note how little attention the cops paid to the systematic harassment that occurred in the years before the kidnapping, not to mention how little they investigated the kidnapping.

Wynette was suffering for decades from addiction, abuse, and trauma—trauma compounded by a music industry that disregarded women's professional roles. Everything we know about the kidnapping, every theory and consideration is complicated by these three factors. Even if it was faked as part of a publicity stunt, it was done under these constant pressures. That this central point in Wynette's career is under-considered suggests that Wynette herself has been under-considered. This event has been dismissed as a kind of lark, with a refusal to acknowledge the ongoing harassment that occurred before this moment. Even the police, who were willing to look the other way, suggested that Wynette wasn't considered reliable. McDonough quotes the journalist Alanna Nash, who wrote that "Wynette was obviously somebody who was very self-destructive, a person who needed to cause a lot of chaos in her life, a lot of drama."[25] The tone of McDonough in his section on the kidnapping shows that he believes Wynette faked it, and that she also faked the other violence that marred her life at this time. This loud, messy, public incident is the first time that she really broke, that she made public the maelstrom of her life. That is one of the consequences of making the private public.

The kidnapping marks what we cannot (or refuse to) know about Wynette, even in her prime.

SEX

Tammy Wynette's album covers, for most of her career, were temperature gauges for how she was feeling, via a range of glamorous self-portraits. The images often said less about the music inside and more about Wynette herself. Fans could draw conclusions about who she was at a given moment in her career by looking at her latest album cover. There was the left-leaning head shot, emphasizing her awkward nose and swan neck, on 1967's *Your Good Girl's Gonna Go Bad* (the awkwardness suggesting someone who is new enough not to be fully integrated into the Nashville machine). The straight-on, almost confrontational approach, with the beehive helmet, on 1969's *Stand By Your Man*. The split double portrait of her and Jones, kind of like a redneck version of Ingmar Bergman's *Persona*, on 1973's *We're Gonna Hold On*. The Vaseline-smeared, far-off gaze shared by her and Jones on 1976's *Golden Ring*.

Then came 1978's *Womanhood*.[1] From the front cover onward, the album indicates something strange, and something new. Part of this novelty is a move away from the modesty of the albums before Jones and during their marriage, as well as the familial image presented by the covers with him. This is an album cover that declares her singleness. She's in a low-cut, sleeveless black gown, showing more skin than ever before. It's a sleek and sophisticated number, something urbane. This isn't the concert wear or even the kind of Nashville brocade that would be seen on the other covers. It reads more New York than anywhere south of the Mason-Dixon line. She looks good, spare and luxe at the same time.

What aren't luxe, and are almost shocking, are her face and her hair. Her face is crumpled in what looks like genuine sorrow. She has a nude lip, and her eyes are wet. Her eye makeup is expertly applied, but looks smudged and slightly faded: not smeared, but not fully present. Lastly, in a moment against vanity, she has a pile of blonde hair on her head, not carefully teased but as sloppy as Wynette would allow.

It's obviously a wig. Before this moment, Wynette's hair and Wynette's wig had been carefully integrated. One was never sure where the real hair ended and the fake hair began. That was the fusion of hair and wig, of the "real" and the "artificial." They were brought together to fulfill a singular purpose. But this album cover, with its sophisticated dress and its otherwise seamless aesthetic, shows a moment where the hair and the wig can be told apart. It's symbolic, subtle at first but jarring when paid attention to.

It's jarring because her image advertised her music and her music/image provided context for her personal life, the covers foregrounding Wynette as part of a cluster — newly married to George Richey, she was no longer single, no longer a singles artist. Wynette's marriage to Jones had lasted six years; she had recorded six albums with him during the marriage. She released five albums between their 1975 divorce and 1978's *Womanhood*. Wynette was nothing if not productive, pumping out product. The albums right after Jones are the usual kind of heartbreak albums. Their covers reflect a generic kind of sadness that we expect of Wynette. For all her success in commercializing and aestheticizing heartbreak, we never got a *Phases and Stages*[2] or a *Blood on the Tracks*[3] from Wynette, no concept album about her divorce that tells its stories with plain talk, heartbreak, and perhaps even anger. Her heartbreak albums by this time stay in one space while the culture moves on.

The whole *Womanhood* album tenses between her putting herself together and falling apart. It's a masterpiece of self-creation in which the sign and the signifier, the labor of public presentation and the gap in social power, are found in a single shot. The cover photo was taken by Norman Seeff, which indicates another shift in the persona. Seeff was known mostly for large-scale, long, yet quite intimate sessions in Los Angeles, first at his studio on the Sunset Strip, then later in a home studio further up in the hills. Though the shoot for the cover was most likely not done in either studio, the fact that Wynette was willing to work with Seeff and that the final image shows the seams in her public persona tells of a move away from Nashville.

For all of the album's visual novelty, its sound was an extension of her previous style to an almost baroque level; the factory quality was made so slick it could have been extruded. It was a Wynette album, but it was a Wynette album that was at the edges of what a Wynette album could be. These edges are indicated by the sales. The album didn't sell badly, but it didn't sell well either. After the song "Womanhood," she would never again have a top ten hit, and the top twenty hits were thin on the ground. The album also wasn't reviewed widely, and when it was reviewed, it wasn't reviewed well. But not always. A semi-anonymized reviewer identified only as N.C., writing in *Stereo Review*, had this perspective: "These are not mostly token songs but real ones, engaging enough to engage Tammy. And when that happens, you hear in her the oddest mixture of toughness and vulnerability."[4]

There is Tammy, the bored professional; Tammy, who is willing to give it a go; and then Tammy, who is able to put on tenderness, even though the idea that one must be real to find meaning in work is still in play. This is not an odd mix, it's her job, but it's one that critics had trouble deconstructing. If great art was made in country music, it was as the result of hard work. The pace of putting out one or two albums a year—reliable and low key—made for a different understanding of labor. If some of the songs weren't great, that was less of a crisis than if they didn't sell well. And if they weren't great *and* didn't sell well, it was all right as long as they weren't part of a bad streak.

There are songs on this album that are too lush, almost strangled by strings. Released within months of Willie Nelson's *Stardust*,[5] the production on *Womanhood* marked the album as old-fashioned at best. *Stardust*, an album of standards—flirting with the past, the crooning and the fingerpicking—could have sounded dated. It doesn't sound timeless; it has the ennui of the late 1970s, the wide spaces and weariness of Terrence Malick's movies or Robert Adams's photography. But Nelson translated dated material to contemporary forms, something that Wynette's codependence with Sherrill made impossible.

Starting with 1968's "D-I-V-O-R-C-E" and ending with "Womanhood," together Wynette and Sherrill produced a decade of hits and a decade of heartbreak. The difference between a good Sherrill song and a bad Sherrill song is complicated. The songs had a machine-hewed shine, a consistency of purpose, and the mark of labor. Wynette knew this, so when she sang, she gave her best, and Sherrill gave his best on production. There were no bad songs. There were songs that didn't work as well, songs that were less semantically rich, songs that were novelties or throwaways, but none that were clunkers. Which means that what one looks for with Sherrill are songs that stand out because of an excellent performance, a reading that makes sense given the culture, songs whose writing is stark or spare, production that is especially interesting, or, to be frank, work that is just a little weird.

The album's two singles, "Womanhood" and "I'd Like to See Jesus (On the Midnight Special)," and also "The One Song I Never Could Write" — one of the great depictions of fame from any artist — are excellent, weird, and as lovely as anything else in Wynette's catalog. They indicate a fascinating break with her usual performative femininity. There are also great songs about the majestic power of sad songs — for example, "You Oughta Hear the Song" — and at least one ode to voyeurism, "Love Doesn't Always Come (On the Night It's Needed)."

"Womanhood"[6] was written by Bobby Braddock, who was tight with Sherrill and was a well-known hitmaker who knew the history of Wynette's life. Working in concord with Wynette, Braddock made a set of rhetorical arguments about what marriage is — both her marriage and marriage in general. For example, the chorus of that earlier hit, "D-I-V-O-R-C-E,"[7] written by Braddock and Curly Putman, starts with the statement "Our divorce becomes final today," an in media res depiction of the failure of love. The voice grinds against some of the dense production. As in "I Don't Wanna Play House," the addition of a child into the heartbreak complicates the narrative and deepens the domestic discord.

"Womanhood" isn't the last song Braddock and Wynette worked on together, but it works as a bookend to "D-I-V-O-R-C-E." If "D-I-V-O-R-C-E" was a woman arguing with a man for fidelity that he finds impossible to give, then "Womanhood" was a woman convincing herself that fidelity might be over-considered. In discussing "Womanhood" in his autobiography, *Bobby Braddock: A Life on Nashville's Music Row*, Braddock tells about how his wife, Susan Lawrence (whom he nicknamed Sparky), rescued the song from the trash and about how the song tells of a girl who is begging God to allow her to no longer be a virgin.[8]

Though Braddock is mostly correct, for complex reasons women's stories ebb and flow in Nashville, and in 1978 there was a major flow. I also find it interesting that even with his paragraph-long discussion of the song, he claimed that he had enough songs that he could have thrown away a great one. That Sparky Lawrence, one of the few women in the RCA Studios, could have fished the song out of a trash can and noticed its greatness is an elegant gender flip.

What's strange to me is that Braddock considered the song's speaker to be an adolescent. Wynette often sang through the voices of children, but they were young children: toddlers, or at the most (in "I Don't Wanna Play House") turning five years old. Wynette's songs about sex, however, were songs about adults and sex, and her songs about desire and hunger were often about a hunger for other people's husbands, and her sorrowful songs were often about being cheated on herself. With all due respect to Braddock, the song has a subtext he's avoiding.

Adultery is one of country's great themes — as heartbreak, as pleasure, as hunger, as a resolved problem, and as a destabilizing force. If Braddock had given this song to a younger and less sophisticated performer, the reading he proposes in his book could hold weight. But Wynette, after years of singing about adultery and hunger, is singing here about how to be a woman, how to fail as a woman, and how to be believed. There is no other way to read this song within this performance than as one about an adult woman who uses her gender to make difficult choices, including the choice to step out on her husband.

All of that complexity is in the vocals. "Womanhood" begins with a solid, intimidating guitar — almost like a train — and then breaks open with a pedal steel. The song centers on Bill Justis's lurid string orchestrations, instrumentation that Sherrill had included with most of Wynette's work, but it's dense with an almost desperate forward momentum in this song. When Wynette's voice enters, it sounds nearly broken, slower than the instrumentation but trying to catch up, almost stumbling over itself, reinforcing that desperation. About halfway through the track, other voices emerge. The first is a man's voice, deep and resonant, encouraging her to do what she wants to do; the next, a whole choir, is a kind of devilish mirror of a heavenly one.

The chorus features the Nashville Edition, a studio vocal group as prolific as any of its peers and marked by a ruthless efficiency. The Edition sang on almost twelve thousand recordings in its lifetime, sometimes working up to four sessions a day. The closely harmonizing voices of these singers carried a professional sleekness.[9]

The Nashville Edition sang a lot of gospel songs, and the introduction of the choir almost sanctifies an unholy moment here. The chorus underlines this juxtaposition between the sacred and the profane with Wynette singing,

> I am a Christian, Lord, but I'm a woman too.
> If you are listenin', Lord, please show me what to do.
> I've tried hard to be what mama says is good
> As I slip into my womanhood.

There is so much in this chorus, so much that is certainly country and so much that is centrally Wynette, that I don't think it should be heard as a song about a teenager losing her virginity. The first lines present it as a character song, rhyming "Patricia" with "kiss ya," awkwardly. Considering the kinds of songs that Wynette sang, and the ambivalence between her personal and professional lives, though this song is in character, listening to its ardor — it reads as a song about fucking outside of marriage.

One of the central themes of Wynette's career was how "it's hard to be a woman," and by extension it's hard to avoid the traps that exist in performing womanhood. Wynette's singing claims authorship over Braddock's words in how it argues for splitting the difference between the personas — between the pious woman and the slut. If "Your Good Girl's Gonna Go Bad" is a threat against a man that by extension destabilizes a heterosexual marriage, then this is permission seeking from the Divine, not against anyone but toward a woman's own liberation.

This was the era when books like *Fascinating Womanhood*, often sold to evangelical women, talked to women about making themselves sexually available to their husbands: to depart from the prim and proper qualities that had been imposed on women, but to do so only in order to save their husbands.[10] It was a response to the sexual liberation of the decade — arguing for a new kind of sexual liberation that should exist only in service of one person and one marriage, an ironic and conservative sexual liberation. In this song, Wynette splits the concepts of Christian and Woman. She's responding to this cultural phenomenon, but she can't imagine going along with it. Maybe the protagonist isn't married, or maybe she's in a dead marriage. (The song claims to be about "Patricia," but like many of Wynette's songs, it's at once about a character, about Wynette, and about the current social and political climate.) The singer can't imagine reconciling her sexuality, her selfhood, and her religion, so she asks permission from the Lord to perform womanhood; that performance can best be described as a kind of nonnormative or nonprescriptive sex. She doesn't say directly, "Jesus, let me fuck a man who isn't my husband," but she does say "as I step into my womanhood" in a throaty, smoky alto, in a torchsong range; what she says and how she says it hint at moral complexity.

Stepping into one's womanhood, slipping into one's womanhood in order to seduce a man, is an acknowledgment of how much of a costume gender is, a double entendre: with an emphasis on slippery, the womanhood here is one intended as pleasurable. That the song pleads to God to allow her this shift complicates Wynette's ideas of pleasure and how it connects to gender. Womanhood seems vexed on the surface, but when she slips into that gender, there is a euphoria that overwhelms any other reading.

The album *Womanhood* was Wynette's last masterpiece — and its strengths go beyond the title track. When she sings "You Oughta Hear the Song"[11] in sweet, soft tones, with a muted drum and a quiet piano, what emerges is a track about the power of music, as well as the emotional devastation of nostalgia. The match between feeling and singing here is profoundly simple, made even more so by the clever moves from singing in the verse, to a chorus of da-da-das, to an old-school recitation.

The delightfully meta "The One Song I Never Could Write"[12] has a killer chorus, with the classic lines

> I got fans who adore me
> Bankers who bore me
> They hear every song
> That I write.

Just as Wynette is deeply aware of her high femme performance in the title track, these two songs talk about how effective country music can be—at reveling in a lover, expressing heartbreak—but also about the failures of that music: it can provide awards and money, but the narrator still is left alone. She has this hope that the saddest song she's ever heard will make someone else sad, but she can't even remember that song. The album's ambivalence about her role in the new Nashville, about the failures of womanhood, of singing, of memory, and of desire, distinguishes it as one of the most vexed Wynette recordings.

The other single released from the album is just batty, but charmingly batty, not to mention theologically messy. It's one of my favorite vocal performances, mostly for the tender and intertextual way Wynette sings the titles of hymns she loves. "I'd Like to See Jesus (On the Midnight Special)"[13] is a song about seeking the return of Christ, but that return does not involve the raising of the dead, nor the embodiment of the second coming. It's about Jesus being a guest on *The Midnight Special*, the radio show hosted by Wolfman Jack:

> I'd like to see Jesus, on the Midnight Special,
> I'd like to see the Wolfman bring him on.
> I'd like to see Jesus, on the Midnight Special,
> That's what it's gonna take to turn the whole world on.

I have no idea how to parse these lines, no idea of the theological implications of them, but I like the idea of Jesus as a guest on a radio show. In the 1960s and 1970s, *turn on* could mean both drug-induced illumination and sexual thrill, giving the whole thing a frisson of decadent pleasure. Sort of like Kris Kristofferson's "Jesus Was a Capricorn," but instead of a lover of organic food, this is a Jesus who knows the average Sunday hymn lineup at a Baptist church in the South from the 1950s to the 1970s. It wraps an understanding of the cosmic in the very local.

That's one of the keys to Wynette—the music being meta, knowing its place, being conscious of its desires, asking for what it wants, and not being surprised when it can't get it. Wynette's aim is always toward ambivalence, a kind of haunted hunger for a selfhood that is never stable, and rarely self-perpetuating.

FAME

Tammy Wynette and George Jones were together for six miserable years and produced six albums during that time, plus three more released later on. Their albums sold well and were deeply respected. The albums were about difficult relationships. Oddly, for a married couple, they tended to record music that was about heartbreak, loss, or infidelity more often than about love, or mutual affection, or desire, or continence. The album cuts occasionally mention devotion, but there are few traditional love songs.

Their albums during this time were not about fame, they were to convince the working-class audience that they loved each other very much and that that love was deeply ordinary. The tension between these two spaces, fame and ordinariness, estranged and isolated the two—the audience wanted to buy that they were just folks, and Wynette and Jones also wanted the audience to believe that. The melodrama that existed in these albums and singles could be understood as an expression of the political reality of the time. Wynette and Jones's fame paradoxically gave them the moral authority to be plain. This plainness could be centered on these two, with plausible deniability with regard to the larger politics.

Their substantial list of songs that worked out the personal as public could include their first single, "Take Me," from *We Go Together*,[1] about "going to the darkest room" and bolting themselves inside or going to the "most barren desert" — about a love that could not occur in public but must be taken to the extreme edges of the landscape. Their second album, *Me and the First Lady*,[2] features the self-apparent "Lovely Place to Cry" and one of the great divorce ballads (yes, on their second album, just three years into their marriage), "Great Divide." Their fourth album, *Let's Build a World Together*,[3] contains what would become two anthems: "After the Fire Is Gone," not a great success for Wynette and Jones (it only hit number thirty-two), but an earlier number one for Loretta Lynn and Conway Twitty; and "My Elusive Dreams," a song over the top in its sadness, a piling up of tragedies, that gets so bathetic around the chorus that it becomes an excellent example of accidental camp. The sixth album, *George and Tammy and Tina*,[4] features the self-descriptive "We're Putting It Back Together" (spoiler alert: they didn't) and "God's Gonna Get-cha (For That)" (which sounds like a comedy song but was sung in earnest — ironically, because it's probable that both of them were cheating). The seventh album, *Golden Ring*,[5] the first one they made after their marriage ended in 1975, features the O. Henry–style title song, which begins in a pawn shop and ends in a pawn shop with a divorce in between. They released two albums after this, one in 1980 and one in 1995.[6]

Jones and Wynette's string of duets was typical of the time — though a little squarer. The 1970s were rife with duets. Lynn and Twitty, for example, recorded ten albums together. They were not married, but their work had a charm that was genuinely erotic: it was often about lovers divided by geography ("Mississippi Woman/Louisiana

Man") or circumstances (the heartbreak anthem "As Soon as I Hang Up the Phone"). I know I believed that Twitty and Lynn were fucking (even if they weren't) and were sad about not fucking later. Wynette's work with Lynn, though lacking the eroticism of Lynn's songs with Twitty, had a profound tenderness. They spent a lot of time together, and they had had a similar economic and social model growing up — the warmth that infuses their best duets has a filial energy. The work with Jones is different. There is tenderness and sadness, often an overwhelming melancholy, but it's music that seems convinced of its own legend and often, distantly, of its genre — country music about country music — and this distance means that the ardor, or the fondness, is placed at arm's length to other, more meta concerns.

It's miraculous that Wynette and Jones had the ability to push through so much material, most of it good, some of it even at the apex of their genre, in the middle of such a chaotic marriage. Drowning in a sea of alcohol, songs that could have been written as sad or angry were rewritten as low comedy, as broad parodies of the marital spats that occurred in songs within the genre, and that both Wynette and Jones had witnessed growing up. Jones was born in Saratoga, Texas, one of seven children, and his father was a drunk. Though Jones didn't provide many details in his autobiography, it's known that his father beat him and that there was severe emotional abuse.[7] One of the things Jones had in common with Wynette was they both grew up early. They didn't have enough time to just be children and to learn how to live as adults. They also might not have had time to unlearn the lessons from the instability of their own raising. Even with Jones, the slippery nature of the ideas of playing house and living together, performing marriage for each other and for an audience that overcommitted to a set of romantic delusions, must have led to some chaos. This chaos did not exclude Jones's violence or instability. In fact, personally and professionally, Jones was much less stable than Wynette.

For example, Wynette always showed up to gigs; Jones did not. One week in early 1973, Jones missed six days of gigs and no one knew where he'd gone. They called his manager, songwriter friends, and other singers, with no luck, and the anxiety ratcheted up. He eventually showed up on his sister's porch in Beaumont, Texas, with no memory whatsoever of where he'd been. Things got even more complicated when Wynette and Jones were in the same place. There is an infamous story in which Jones gets apocalyptically drunk at a performance and is taken home. Wynette and her employee (which employee, no one really knows) bring him into the house and try to get him into bed. He convinces himself that Wynette is leaving for good, and as she exits the bedroom he finds a firearm and goes after her. She starts screaming and races out the door. She runs down the street until she finds a phone, where she calls a private detective she keeps on retainer. Cliff Hyder, a former neighbor, had moved but is visiting the couple. For most of the rest of the evening, Wynette, Hyder, and the detective hide in the bushes, listening to Jones completely trash their home.[8]

There was economic and social pressure to stay together. The albums sold well, and the concert tours sold better. But after stories like this, one wonders whether the work was worth it, whether the money was worth it, and whether the material was worth it.

Wynette and Jones's 1973 album *We're Gonna Hold On*[9] includes the happiest of their songs together, "(We're Not) The Jet Set." The song's happiness seems a little desperate, perhaps trying to convince the audience of a joy that might be performative. The highlight of the album is a cover of Flatt and Scruggs's tight harmonic updating of the nineteenth-century ballad "Roll in My Sweet Baby's Arms," perhaps the sexiest that Wynette and Jones ever were. There's a really great, funny, late version of this from a London concert in the early 1980s,[10] when all the rancor has burnt off and they're just affectionate with each other—an affection that reveals some of the charisma and proves that their love wasn't entirely tragic.

Jones and Wynette's best songs can read like jokes, but they're rarely funny. Think of "Two Story House,"[11] about how one couple's real estate ambitions fail to shore up their collapsing marriage. The story in this song combines the dual narratives of the lovers, but if the punchline in these story songs is about the split between expectations and what is delivered, the gap is a gap of sadness. This kind of sad or tragic punchline reflects that, at least as a couple, Jones and Wynette didn't have a sense of humor about themselves. The odd thing about this is that they were each hyperaware of their own persona. They knew how to craft stories about themselves for their audience, and both were fantastic at stage banter, ingratiating themselves with crowds that wanted the mix of glamour and down-homeness that was expected of country superstars. They knew how to sell, and knew who they were, but they were severe. (Of course, severity and humor are not mutually exclusive. No one was more severe than Johnny Cash, but he was secure enough in his Jeremiah persona that he took the piss out of it on the regular. See, for example, his appearance on *Sesame Street* singing "Nasty Dan" to Oscar the Grouch,[12] or his song "The Chicken in Black," a goofy story song where Cash's brain was replaced first with that of a bank robber, then that of a chicken — recorded to get out of a bad Columbia contract in the mid-1980s.[13])

"(We're Not) The Jet Set"[14] is one of the few examples of Wynette and Jones having fun. Instead of doubling down on the sadness or exhaustion of being so aware of their personas, they seem to revel joyfully in that awareness. Even more surprising, Billy Sherrill, who by the late 1970s had developed slightly hidebound habits in producing Wynette's sound, treated the music of "Jet Set" in a way that heightened the parody. Beginning with a fluttering string section that matches the exoticism of the lyrics, the song floats in on a cloud of perfumed air: the duo recount the romantic settings — "a fountain back in Rome," "a small cafe in Athens," "April in Paris" — where they first "fell in love."[15]

Then, following the revelation that they mean "Rome, Georgia; Athens, Texas; and Paris, Tennessee," the song drops into a honky-tonk groove. There is an exaggerated bounce to the pedal steel, underlining a genuine gag. Country, in this period, had a particular imperative to perform working-class consciousness. The song is a funny joke, but ironically, it's a defense of an aesthetic that was still the butt of jokes. Also ironically, it never quite made it into the country canon. It sold okay, reaching number fifteen on the country charts, but not as well as much of Jones and Wynette's other work.[16]

In his essay "Class Unconsciousness in Country Music,"

the critic Richard A. Peterson places "(We're Not) The
Jet Set" in a genre he calls "poverty pride." Peterson discusses how in commercial country music from the 1960s
to the 1980s, noting Wynette and Jones specifically, the
songs prioritize regional identities over a generalized idea
of class; they center on a specific working-class southern
identity, and a white one at that, over the solidarity that
might come from a wider or more complex class identity. One was proud of being working class, but one was
prouder of being from the South, or, even more locally,
from a town or a hollow, or even just holding the idea of
home. Peterson then provides a canon, starting in 1961,
with Bill Anderson's "Po' Folks"; moving on to Loretta
Lynn's "Coal Miner's Daughter"; Merle Haggard's "Hun-
gry Eyes," "Roots of My Raising," and "Mama Tried";
and Dolly Parton's "Coat of Many Colors" and "Chicken
Every Sunday."[17] Of course, these songs are by artists who
have already made it. Making it out of poverty gives performers permission to be nostalgic about hard childhoods.

   Written in the midst of an economic crisis, "(We're Not)
The Jet Set" is a recontextualization of an era of massive
social change. The songs Peterson mentions are in part
about the re-entrenchment of the South—a white push-
back against the rise of Black cultural power. There are
songs that are ironic, or winking, or messy in their inten-
tion—see Haggard's "Okie from Muskogee,"[18] which is a
joke, and a serious history of his youth, and a character
study, and a political moment, and all of these things or
none of these things. "Jet Set" is part of this overall pattern. Jones and Wynette are making an explicit argument
in favor of region and place, as a legitimate source of

culture, a joke at their own expense but also one in which the insider can kid around and play. The outsider can't do the same thing. This kind of joke reinforces the interiority of a community and imposes its will against interlopers.

"Jet Set" is a song in defense of taste, an aesthetic argument as much as a political or social one. When Chuck Berry sang "Roll over Beethoven, tell Tchaikovsky the news," he was arguing in favor of the legitimacy of his form; when Wynette and Jones argue in favor of Haggard and Husky, an ethic and an aesthetic merge into one idea of taste.

For Jones and Wynette, an American conception of taste is central. Singing about being a member of "the Chevrolet set" is engaging in a social contract of taste, the aesthetic/ethic being an all-American one, and in particular a southern one. Wynette and Jones manage expectations, carefully. It's a joke song, but one with an explicit social message.

The singer-songwriter Robbie Fulks surfaces those barely hidden tensions in his reworking of "Jet Set." Fulks's song choices always hover between the insidery wink and the outsider's contempt. His 2013 live cover of "Jet Set" at the alt-country/folk club the Hideout in Chicago, with the folk singer Jodee Lewis, has a post-ironic snark. Fulks introduces it by saying he's going to try not to sing it sentimentally though he is down with sentiment. Thinking that the least sentimental Bobby Braddock song is sentimental is Fulks's first problem, and is such a rookie mistake it's hard to believe he isn't fucking with us. When he sings the word *Paris*, he stretches the second vowel into Rudy Vallee territory. In fact, he adds his own verse, at the very end, one that compares an urban elite's "Whole

Foods" and "gay pride" to the working-class South's "no school" and "hay rides."[19] Those eight words dismantle the working-class regional pride of the rest of the song.

One of the central goals of the original song was to push back against those who mock southerners, making the inside jokes and the self-consciously ironic Nashville identities into something wider. Jones and Wynette's wasn't the genial "aw shucks" humanism of someone like President Jimmy Carter, and it was also not the explicit and precise local and class representation that was attempted by those in the Outlaw country scene. The cities mentioned in "Jet Set" were more like symbolic ideas of a place; they weren't doing the reportage of something like Waylon Jennings's "Luckenbach, Texas,"[20] which tells of an actual physical location where, "with Waylon and Willie and the boys," musicians can escape the economic and social pressures of road life.

Wynette sang mostly about home — "Jet Set" is an obvious exception, but her ability to fold the domestic into the wider world is key to understanding this song as well. There is a similar trick found in Lynn's work, though Lynn was spikier. Lynn didn't really care if she was liked, and that attitude made her more attractive to city sophisticates. City folks in general, and New Yorkers specifically, can appreciate a good "fuck you." But Wynette wanted to be liked. Wynette sang about motherhood, about heartbreak, about desire, and about the preservation of the heterosexual mode at a time when women's domestic sphere was continually being dismissed by radicals and exploited by reactionaries. Both singers worked on behalf of those considered the "silent majority" (even though they were not the majority and they were not silent). Lynn's "One's on the Way"[21] could be read in concordance with "(We're Not) The Jet Set." They're both comical songs, both songs about life in the South, and both defenses of working-class ideals, and both position those modes as worthy against the seemingly superior sophistication of the outside world. Lynn talks about who exactly the Chevrolet set might be, contrasting them with New York women's libbers, the upwardly mobile publishers of *Better Homes and Gardens*, and the sexually liberated users of the birth-control pill:

> But here in Topeka, the rain is a fallin',
> The faucet is a drippin' and the kids are a bawlin',
> One of 'em a toddlin' and one is a crawlin'
> And one's on the way.

Lynn didn't live the life she sang about, which is fine, assuming closely drawn parallels between biography and art are unnecessary and possibly even foolish. However, if you're singing about being a plain, working-class person while very rich, the gap should be noticed. Lynn supported Trump, and there is an analogue here, in the thinking that Trump's supporters were poor or working-class people when in fact many of them were part of the haute bourgeois managerial classes. The nostalgic heritage of what one was never replaces what one is.

This was one problem of the postwar boomers, under Nixon, one of the most financially successful generations in history, who claimed to be the silent majority while crafting lives that excluded poor people, queer folks, and people of color. They needed to believe they were both hard done by and nothing like anyone who genuinely was. Their political imagination was accompanied by a political will that excluded these groups of people.

The critic Richard Goldstein, writing about country music in *Mademoiselle* in 1973, claimed that "country music comes equipped with a very specific set of values which include . . . political conservatism, strongly differentiated male and female roles, a heavily punitive racism . . . and rugged individualism."[22] This isn't wrong, entirely, especially about gender roles, and duets like "Jet Set" suggest both a couple (as opposed to an individual) and a whole set of people (an economic and social class) who built an infrastructure to continue the legal exclusion of Black people in the South. Wynette had the racial politics expected of a person of her station, geographic region, and era, and her marriages never upended patriarchal conventions, but how she sang about men was codependent more than it was ever individualistic.

Wynette's signature voice made it difficult for people to cover her, and for her to cover other people. But there's an opposites-attract delight in how well John Prine covered Wynette's songs, "Jet Set" most famously, and in how Wynette covered Prine's "Unwed Father." Her version takes up the pointed irony of Prine's piercing story song about fathers who "run like a mountain stream." Wynette, in 1983, returned the alt-country from the 1970s back to Nashville, telling the audience, and perhaps Prine, that for all their hipness, they were working melodrama just like she was. Prine's singing "Jet Set" and Wynette's singing "Unwed Fathers" argued for a mutual interest in storytelling about a very specific kind of place.[23]

Prine wrote and sang about a different kind of south, though he came closer than other country singers to claiming Wynette's world for his own. He wrote intensely about the landscape, what was lost, and the isolation of small-town living. His "Paradise"[24] is a song about how toxic nostalgia can be and about how the landscape had been destroyed by the coal companies, the labor done in Kentucky a kind of ecocide.

There is no one better than Prine at reflecting the tenderness, the performative quality, and the almost irony that "(We're Not) The Jet Set" allows. Prine sang the song with the folk singer Iris DeMent on an album of duets.[25] Iris DeMent's and Tammy Wynette's performances are both earnest, but DeMent's earnest qualities are haunted and radical, an unadorned far-left progressiveness — qualities not shared by Wynette. The song begins with a wavering steel guitar. Then you hear DeMent's voice, and her joking quality makes the song stronger — it undercuts her usual seriousness and advances the story. It's a careful reading of Wynette and Jones. One of the things it does very well, perhaps better than the original, is note that this is a love song. The question comes up, when writing about Wynette and Jones, of whether they actually loved each other, whether they had any tenderness toward each other at all. Prine was a tender singer, and one who believed deeply in love. This tender version answers for Wynette: of course she and Jones loved each other, despite the chaos of their lives, and this makes the track one of the great love songs.

The last line of the chorus of "Jet Set" is "But ain't we got love." It's the most sentimental line in the whole song. When Prine and DeMent sing it, the love is platonic — there's deep fondness but not really the frisson of desire. But with Jones and Wynette, "Jet Set" is the song that explains why they might have loved each other: they never stepped on each other's lines or stole the punchline. Wynette and Jones sang like they loved each other. They were masters at selling all the ways of loving someone, from new infatuation to heartbreak. Listening to their music, and just their music, one can be convinced that a marriage of less than a decade could be one of country music's greatest love stories. But what kind of a love story features a man beating his wife, and how many love stories are about a woman convincing herself that being beaten is a measure of being loved? Using the word *passion* to describe Wynette and Jones's relationship, as an explanation for the fights, the screaming, the late-night drinking, the mistaking of abuse for love—that is a country-music problem. It's the commercially convenient myth that the life is the work. The problem is that Wynette and Jones made such genius work that the confusion is understandable.

No matter how sad "He Stopped Loving Her Today" is, it must be remembered that she stopped loving him while he was still alive. And no matter how funny "Jet Set" is, it should be remembered that Tammy Wynette wasn't spending a lot of time consuming draft beer with wieners.

TRADITION

Authenticity is bullshit, and tradition is bullshit, but in Nashville this bullshit is where a lot of flowers grow. As with all growing cycles, there are bumper crops — and the mid-1970s anxieties between various factions of country music gave us a bumper crop. There were the slightly out-of-season Countrypolitan singers and the California musicians of two varieties — the hard-playing honky-tonking of Bakersfield and the soft slowness of the Eagles or Gram Parsons, who cross-pollinated with Texans as diverse as Emmylou Harris or Linda Ronstadt. There was a crop of Austin musicians who pretended their roots were local instead of in Tennessee, and then there was a set of invading species, from Colorado (John Denver) or Australia (Olivia Newton-John), among other places. In 1975, when Waylon Jennings sang "Are You Sure Hank Done It This Way," the assumption was that Hank did not do it this way — the "it" being the soft rock of Denver or Newton-John, winners of CMA awards around the same time Jennings won one. What was country then? Was it soft rock, was it the rock and roll that George Jones was forging, was it Willie Nelson's complex reworkings of Tin Pan Alley songs, was it the obscene and liberated inner geographies of David Allan Coe's working-class

Souths, was it Dolly Parton starting to become Hollywood or Loretta Lynn's working-class irascibility, or was it Johnny Cash singing about trains, Charley Pride singing about cotton, or Freddie Fender singing in Spanish?

Country was all of these things and none of these things, and how you answered the question showed not only an aesthetic or social affiliation but a political one as well. Tammy Wynette's recording of *Womanhood* in 1978 sort of marked her as traditional but also argued in favor of the continued importance of Sherrill and his Countrypolitan style. The tradition wasn't the rejection of the studio sheen found in some of the back-to-the-land folkies, but it also wasn't the smoothness of the soft rock crowd. To place Wynette in context, it's helpful to consider the work of Dolly Parton in the 1970s as she was negotiating between various kinds of tradition and novelty—singing Appalachian ballads in Hollywood and singing Hollywood songs on ad hoc stages near canals in East Tennessee.

Parton worked as a fulcrum for Wynette's recordings in other ways as well. There were two significant trios that Parton was involved in from the mid-1970s to the mid-1990s. The questions of taste and of what exactly country music could be were at the center of the work of both of these groupings. The first trio was with Linda Ronstadt and Emmylou Harris and resulted in the album *Trio* in 1987. These three women worked together as early as 1976, near the height of both Ronstadt's and Parton's success but close to the beginning of Harris's career. However, the combination of different record labels, punishingly busy schedules, and far-separated home bases meant the significant recording didn't happen until the mid-1980s.[1]

One of the results of the early sessions is a 1976 performance on Parton's 1970s variety show, *Dolly*. Since it was Parton's show, this performance is mostly hers. She sings two full verses of "Silver Threads and Golden Needles" before Harris and Ronstadt come in from the wings. The three of them then sing one chorus. Parton, slightly awkward but with full charm, introduces her guests and they all sing another chorus together.[2] Their performance on the show suggests that the song had become a set of interlocking choruses prioritizing harmonies, where the verses retreat into the background and the choruses sound better with a leader rather than as a genuine trio performance.

The trio's recording sessions also followed that pattern of cracking apart and then coming back together, with significant cross-pollination in the late 1970s and early 1980s. They recorded and released each other's music as well as music by other singers. Ronstadt would eventually record Parton's "My Blue Tears," and Parton and Ronstadt together recorded the traditional ballad "I Never Will Marry," which ended up on Ronstadt's 1977 album *Simple Dreams*. Parton recorded Harris's "Boulder to Birmingham" for her 1976 album *All I Can Do*. Harris covered Parton's "Coat of Many Colors" and "To Daddy," and Ronstadt recorded Parton's "I Will Always Love You."[3]

These sessions suggested that the group had several things going for it: a free understanding of authorship and property, a willingness to work together, and an agreement on taste being constructed as a kind of connoisseurship. One could argue that these sessions were more of a boon to Harris than to the others, but she provided a new way of looking at country, one that merged history, canons, performing styles, and levels of fame into what would be a decades-long wellspring.

It was a wellspring that gave us an answer about the internecine squabbling of mid-1970s Nashville, a generous both/and agenda that argued against purity but ironically made work that could be read as pure country. This movement away from the tussle and the push, done with Parton as the only genuine star, freed Wynette from a constraining aesthetic. (One can see it continuing to inspire until this decade, with the Miranda Lambert-led group Pistol Annies.)

Dolly's decade-long effort in the first trio, with its performative widening of what country music might mean, proved fecund enough for her to try it a second time. Despite her protestations to the contrary, Parton has always been first among equals — she runs the show but has enough manners to pretend she doesn't. The first trio's album provided the blueprint for the second trio's — *Honky Tonk Angels* (1993)[4] — with, this time, Dolly working alongside Loretta Lynn and Tammy Wynette.

Parton, Lynn, and Wynette had performed together at awards shows and on television specials for a long time, and Parton and Wynette were both affiliated with Porter Wagoner in the 1960s. When they started to record in 1993, Parton was perhaps trying to revive some of the magic from her recordings with Ronstadt and Harris, perhaps doing it as a lark, perhaps doing a favor for some friends. With Wynette's career in the doldrums, and Lynn's on a downhill slide, it made sense for the two to join up with Dolly. I'm not sure Parton's second attempt at a trio worked as well as the first one.

The difference between the trio of Parton, Harris, and Ronstadt and that of Parton, Lynn, and Wynette is telling, especially in terms of country music subgenres. Harris and Ronstadt were committed to a neotraditionalism that ironically denied the need for purity. "Silver Threads and Golden Needles," the song they sang on Parton's show in 1976, is schmaltzy and wasn't on the *Trio* album in 1987, but it is on the album Parton made with Lynn and Wynette in 1993, *Honky Tonk Angels*. There were also differences in singing styles and cohesiveness. The women in the first trio had denser harmonies and were less likely to step on each other's lines. Their voices worked together better. But McDonough isn't wrong when he writes of the second trio, "The down-home camaraderie was palpable and, as Parton explained, unlikely to be seen among their modern counterparts. 'There's a lot of jealousy and competition among a lot of the new singers—it's more like the rock 'n' roll business.'"[5]

Honky Tonk Angels was universally lauded for its beauty, a beauty that doesn't prioritize one vision over anyone else's. It's egoless. Wynette pulls lead on the first (and only) single, "Silver Threads and Golden Needles,"[6] and Lynn and Parton push the harmony. When they performed it at the CMA Awards in 1993, Lynn stepped on one of Wynette's lines and Parton laughed and then explicitly told Lynn to go ahead. This awards-show version is denser and quicker than the one done with Harris and Ronstadt on *Dolly*. It begins with pedal steel before Wynette's distinctive honky-tonk voice cuts through, singing almost the whole first verse alone before Lynn and Parton enter, harmonizing.[7] It's a song where, surprisingly, Lynn and Parton hold back in deference to Wynette.

The music video features a wide range of male suitors, including Chet Atkins and Ronnie Milsap, begging and pushing to get backstage, with Dolly controlling access.[8]

As humorous as the video is, it's also Wynette claiming the power of male voices and making literal the subtext of the song. If the album track prioritizes Wynette's voice, then the video, through a wink and a nod, notices the shifting of gender, where women are in the driver's seat both romantically and in terms of their careers, even in the midst of a downturn for certain legends in the 1990s. The subtext of this performance is twofold: there is an anxiety about money and the consequences of turning down money, especially that which is connected to men; and there is an acknowledgment that for Parton, a kind of solidarity against male power is paramount. This solidarity was easier for them to achieve since Parton had the power to move the levers.

Parton's pushing of the second trio album, when it might have been out of fashion, tells us how very powerful and generous she is. An ungenerous reader could wonder if this album was a bit of a rescue mission. Parton could afford to be gracious because she had the social and economic capital to do what she wanted. She moved in New York and Los Angeles media circles, and she had found a way to have the cornpone, the down home, be read not as a joke or a threat or an example of exoticism but as its own kind of drag, its own kind of ironic self-fashioning. I wonder if Wynette was self-aware enough to note that some people get rewarded for that kind of work and some people get punished for it; I wonder if Wynette felt punished.

Honky Tonk Angels was a nostalgia album, in a slightly old-fashioned honky-tonk style, featuring covers including "It Wasn't God Who Made Honky Tonk Angels," "Lovesick Blues," and "I Dreamed of a Hillbilly Heaven." The album did well critically, nabbing Grammy attention and a CMA award nomination. It also sold well—not as well as Parton's barn burners of the 1980s, but it was eventually certified gold.

Wynette's 1980s albums were a weak spot for her. She seemed bored with her material and unable to break through to do anything different. There was no disco phase, she didn't make an awkward new wave album. She didn't let herself be absorbed into other people's genre experiments (no duos with k.d. lang). She also didn't double down on the nostalgia circuit of county fairs, as many other artists did. For most of the 1980s, Wynette burrowed down deep inside the comfortable space she had built. The 1970s–1980s trio was an act against a singular definition of country music as a genre. The 1990s trio was an act of canon making, reminding an audience of how unassailable these three figures were. If nostalgia has an ache — for lost possibilities, for failed stabs at opportunities — then this album is nostalgic. It's a call for tradition as a call for rest; the singers don't seem bored, but the familiarity gives us less than the almost experimental cross-pollination of the trio with Ronstadt and Harris.

This album could also have been like Johnny Cash's album *American Recordings*, released within a year of *Honky Tonk Angels*. Leaning into his persona, Cash deliberately made an iconic move after a long, slow decade (one in which most of his significant work was with a super group, the Highwaymen). Wynette could have gone darker, could have leaned in to the domestic themes that marked her best work and played the same game Cash did, could have made *Honky Tonk Angels* less of a disappointing lark, but she failed at these as well.

Ronstadt and Harris had a fluid relationship to the authentic and to the traditional — picking and choosing for aesthetic convenience; Cash's approach to tradition was an act of self-monumentalizing. Parton was all things to all people—sometimes country, sometimes disco—but when she returned to the nineteenth century, with "Silver Threads and Golden Needles," it was a deliberate act of dredging cultural and social memory. Lynn's writing managed to paradoxically puncture and maintain very traditional ideas of family. All of these provided examples of how to build tradition around a performance, rather than being constrained by it. *Honky Tonk Angels* was an attempt to follow those examples, but it didn't work as anticipated.

REPRIEVE

Tammy Wynette was anxious about what it meant to be a southern woman in the 1970s, and Burt Reynolds was anxious about what it meant to be a southern man at about the same time. It makes sense that they were lovers for a time during the mid-1970s, and then friends until her death. Both of their careers were filled with ambitious successes and, toward the end of that decade, eccentric failures. Reynolds's machismo was overproduced and over-considered—maybe as a consequence of the civil rights movement, where the ugliness of southern white men was amplified by an anxiety around the loss of power. The idea of the South, of gender in the South, of creating a persona, and of the slippage between what is represented and what is real all exist within both Reynolds and Wynette.

Three films that Reynolds made in the 1970s—*Deliverance*, *Gator*, and *The Longest Yard*—were all, in their way, about men losing power and autonomy in the South and being controlled by the landscape. This is especially true of *Deliverance*, with Reynolds's character literally lost in the Georgia swamps, the "Dueling Banjos" soundtrack making the humiliating violence even worse somehow— the landscape and the music and the violence combining into a total loss of control.[1] For Reynolds in the 1970s, the loss of the South was a total loss of all kinds of control, which makes his 1973 album, *Ask Me What I Am*, a fascinating document of a man in that position.[2]

If we imagine Reynolds to be an example of unrelenting machismo, *Ask Me What I Am* is all about sonic softness. He often doesn't sing on it, reciting or speaking instead, over a bed of pillowy strings. Wynette's explorations of gender are often in code, curtailed or made implicit, but the themes on Reynolds's album are more explicit. Especially in "The First One That I Lay With," a song that lists a variety of past sexual encounters, none of which were consensual. There is also a song, "She's Taken a Gentle Lover," about a woman leaving the (male) narrator for another woman. Wynette could sing about none of these things. Her singing takes all the subtext — the heaviness of desire, the heartbreak of loss, even adultery — and hides it in a production where her voice is only one element. Reynolds's lone album — a kitsch artifact whose two singles failed to chart — rides along on the material, neither engaging nor fully committing.

Perhaps Reynolds's having recorded this album helped bring him and Wynette together. The official story is that the two hooked up in 1976 — in the months between the end of her marriage to Jones and the beginning of her short marriage to the real estate investor Michael Tomlin. She appeared on *The Jerry Reed Show* in September of that year, and she and Burt had dinner together with Reed after the show. A few weeks later, Reynolds called on her while she was recording. The pickers hooted and hollered, making fun of Wynette for having a boyfriend stop by. She and Reynolds would go out. McDonough tells of what they had in common: "Baptist upbringing, a love of country music and the state of Florida."[3] That doesn't seem to have been enough to cement a lasting relationship, but they seemed good for each other. Reynolds had recently been a center-fold in *Cosmopolitan* magazine, and Wynette had a healthy sex drive. That must have been part of it. Also Reynolds wanted more of a recording career than he had, and she could help.

The official biographies have less information about Wynette's paramours outside of her marriages than about her husbands. Elizabeth Taylor joked that she only slept with her husbands; I think the popular idea of Wynette is like that — maybe because it makes it easier to think of her as a victim if she's "pure," maybe because in the conservative Nashville of the time, sexual liberation was limited to male performers. Even after the sex likely ended, Reynolds and Wynette would be friends for the rest of her life.

Burt Reynolds lived in Riviera Beach, Florida, adjacent to West Palm Beach, from the age of ten. Over the course of his adult life, he continued to buy real estate north of there, around Jupiter, despite several financial setbacks and bankruptcies. Reynolds owned a ranch of more than 150 acres in Jupiter Park, just west of Jupiter proper, but sold it during 1999 bankruptcy proceedings. He also built the Burt Reynolds Dinner Theatre in Jupiter in 1979.[4] Wynette appeared at the theater a number of times, including a performance in 1983 with her daughter Tina.

Wynette owned real estate in Florida before she dated Reynolds — a large estate in Lakeland, about two and a half hours northwest of Jupiter, which she bought with Jones and sold in 1972, and the condo in Jupiter that she purchased with Tomlin. We also know that she had ties to a property at Jupiter Inlet Colony in 1980 because she shot the album cover of that year's underperforming *Only Performing Sometimes* there. Wynette's real estate investments in the 1980s resulted in a connection to the savings and loan crisis and an eventual bankruptcy[5]—another parallel between Reynolds and her.

Wynette spent substantial time in the late 1970s and early 1980s in Florida, some of it with Reynolds. She saved him from drowning in her bathtub there, which suggests they enjoyed a degree of domesticity.[6] There is also a story about Loretta Lynn hiding Wynette in her dressing room as Dinah Shore, who was dating Reynolds at the time, was looking for either Wynette or Reynolds.[7] Wynette had to go to the hospital soon after her marriage to Tomlin and McDonough tells us that she asked Reynolds to take her there and that he took care of her in ways Tomlin didn't.[8]

In an attempt to explain away the mess surrounding her lovers in the mid-1970s, she wrote in her autobiography that she wasn't sure who she loved and said she had stated publicly that she loved Tomlin and didn't want to embarrass anyone. Most tellingly, Wynette said that forty-eight hours before her marriage to Tomlin she learned that the *National Enquirer* (another Florida connection) had an exclusive that was supposed to break of the story of her relationship with Reynolds—she might have married Tomlin to cast doubt on their story about Reynolds.[9] Wynette didn't want the public to know about her romance with Reynolds, and the *National Enquirer* was going to print the news of their relationship on its front page. Wynette also thought it was plausible that no one would believe her if she denied the story. She decided to work with the tabloid and not against it, so she married Tomlin. Coe addressed this in one of his podcasts.

According to Tammy, she made the decision to marry Michael about forty-eight hours prior to her lawyer finding out the *National Enquirer* had a cover story coming out on her relationship with Burt Reynolds. According to Tammy, the *Enquirer* was too close to their print deadline to completely change the cover when she announced her engagement to Michael Tomlin and that's why they pivoted at the last minute from a story about Burt Reynolds dating Tammy Wynette to a story about Burt Reynolds dating Tammy Wynette at the same time he was dating Lucie Arnaz, the daughter of Lucille Ball and Desi Arnaz. If you're thinking, "Well, that doesn't really make any sense," no, it doesn't. Especially if you look up when that *National Enquirer* cover story ran and learn it came out three months after Tammy's wedding to Michael, by which time they were already divorced.[10]

One of the challenges of writing about Wynette is that her romantic life and her professional life were sometimes transparent and sometimes occluded, with at times explicit motivations and at other times motivations that are totally lost. Coe is absolutely correct that none of this makes sense. This also suggests that Wynette exercised some power with the tabloids—that she was such good copy, or that at least Reynolds was such good copy, that the exact nature of that copy didn't necessarily matter. For a tabloid in that time and place, trying to figure out who was dating who, who was more famous, and who was better copy, when everyone involved was lying to themselves, their families, each other, and the press, must have been nearly impossible.

Wynette was discreet about Reynolds, affectionate and

almost sweet. Maybe this was because theirs was the only relationship Wynette had where both parties seemed to have the same amount of power and money; there is no evidence of power struggles in the same way that there was with others. There is no evidence that Reynolds hit her. They didn't record together, though they very much could have.

In 1982, Reynolds filmed an adaptation of the Broadway smash *The Best Little Whorehouse in Texas* with Dolly Parton.[11] In it, Dolly plays the madam and Reynolds plays the sheriff who is supposed to shut down the titular whorehouse. There's a song in that movie called "Sneakin' Around," a small and intimate duet about all the little delights of having an affair. Reynolds has such charm, such devotion to pleasure, that the whole thing seems almost wholesome. Wynette, who did a little acting here and there, would have been too uptight and too in her own head to perform the role of the madam, but considering that Reynolds was sneaking around with Wynette, one can see how he might have been a good lay but not a good husband.

Reynolds began dating his costar Sally Field in the late 1970s. He met Field on the set of *Smokey and the Bandit* — a 1977 movie that was less vexed about southernness than *Gator* or especially *Deliverance*. They dated for about five years. Reading about Field's relationship with Reynolds in her memoir makes me think my conclusions on the balance of power in Wynette and Reynolds's relationship might be wishful thinking:

> Burt seemed to wallow in [the pressure of fame], both loving the focus and spinning from its assault. By the time we met, the weight of his stardom had become a way for Burt

to control everyone around him, and from the moment I walked through the door, it was a way to control me. We were a perfect match of flaws. It was instantaneous and intense. Blindly I fell into a rut that had long ago formed in my road, a preprogrammed behavior as if in some past life I had pledged a soul-binding commitment to this man.[12]

Maybe the answer is that Tammy didn't have that soul-binding commitment to Reynolds. They had an intense relationship, and the press was convinced he would ask her to marry him. But they didn't get married, and it's the one great what-if in Tammy's life.[13]

In Wynette's live performances with George Jones, there's a distinct sense of competition — and a stiffness, where the ardor of the performances is tamped down by seriousness or even profound sadness, even during the one or two songs that are supposed to be loose or have a central gag. In the few performances we see of her and Burt Reynolds together, or even the ones of her performing on his home turf, she's as loose as she ever was. I'm thinking especially of one she gave in 1983 at Reynolds's dinner theater, running a little less than ninety minutes. There are covers (a very good one of "Orange Blossom Special," a strange and almost perfunctory "Delta Dawn") and medleys of her greatest hits (including a six-minute one that jam-packs "Your Good Girl's Gonna Go Bad," "Apartment #9," "I Don't Wanna Play House," "D-I-V-O-R-C-E," and "Singing My Song"). But most telling is when she lets her steel guitar player, Charlie Carter, sing Merle Haggard's "Big City."[14] In this song, a man walks off his job in the big, dirty city. He gives up his retirement fund and his "so-called Social Security," saying that after working since he was twenty, he doesn't have anything to show for it. The song is audience bait, and a performer can plug any city into the chorus: "Big City, turn me loose and set me free." Carter seems to be working on behalf of Wynette, and Jupiter is where she wants to be set free. The whole performance is a good time, and this imagining of Jupiter as a respite is central to that entertainment value.[15] The fun must come from being in Florida, and from being on equal footing with Reynolds. Their friendship seems genuine.

When Reynolds was doing his career-reviving Arkansas-set sitcom *Evening Shade*, almost twenty years after the Sturm und Drang of the mid-1970s, he invited Wynette to be on an episode. This was a few years after her success with the KLF, but it also seemed a little bit like a homecoming. K. T. Oslin, a Broadway performer who moved to Nashville and had significant success as a country singer-songwriter before turning to television acting, was also on the episode. Oslin had a complicated relationship to gender and country music: she fully absorbed second-wave feminism but loved old-school country music at the same time; her voice had a small twang and her vocals were wide-ranging with a number of formal influences, including Wynette's. In the nineteenth episode of the fourth season, it almost doesn't matter the plot of the episode, it's a cafe setting and for three minutes the camera focuses on Oslin, who, her head in her hands, isn't looking at Wynette but is listening as Wynette sings a torch song. Oslin then sings her own "sad old love song."[16] It becomes a meta-exercise, a song about songs, a heartbreak about heartbreak, and, inevitably, it's also a song about Wynette. A careful reading of the scene offers deep rewards.

In an interview on set with Reynolds to promote the

show, Wynette is relaxed. They laugh about getting up early and staying up late. She appears to be on intimate terms with Burt as he stumbles to explain his role, and she laughs when he pretends to yell at someone who's making noise on the set—a gag and not a gag. She continues, talking tenderly about how Reynolds very kindly makes suggestions to her when she has "screwed it up royally."[17] In a publicity task for a mediocre sitcom and with more talent than her pat answers would indicate, Wynette slips in a bit of history there—an intimacy that almost forgets the camera.

There is a little bit in the video where Wynette expects or wants to be protected and some old-fashioned chivalry where Reynolds rescues her. He also rescued her from the Clinton-gaffe situation of 1992, partly because of his gallantry and partly because he seemed to return Wynette's own fierce loyalty. As mentioned previously, this is the time when Hillary Clinton tells *60 Minutes* that even if she is staying in her marriage despite her husband's adultery, she's not "standing by [her] man like Tammy Wynette."[18] This craters Hillary Clinton's approval ratings, and she becomes desperate. She calls Wynette's management, and Wynette doesn't respond. They try to get hold of her directly, and she doesn't answer the calls. This becomes a crisis—what to do when the person offended doesn't trust you enough to take your apology? Eventually, someone figures out the Hollywood connection and gets Reynolds to call Wynette. He agrees to do it and also manages to talk her into showing up at a fund-raiser in Beverly Hills, giving the appearance, at least, of having patched things up.[19]

We don't know what that conversation consisted of—how Reynolds convinced Wynette to show up to that fund-raiser. There is a certain kind of access trading and politics here—Wynette knows her value and has to be talked into going. But that she lets Reynolds talk her into it, despite her stated politics, hints at the extreme loyalty they showed to each other.

Wynette and Reynolds had a relationship to the reconsideration of the South—to the politics and geography of the region. Even the use of words such as *gallantry*, or *softness*, or *chivalry* seems to call up images of the South. The performance of gender and geography was central for them both. The irony of their relationship was that despite how public it was, for both of them it was their least public relationship. They made work together, but every other relationship that either of them had been in had connected their business to their lives. In this case, there was no backstage. The most famous person that Wynette loved gave her the quietest relationship she ever had. Watching them together brings up a wistful nostalgia, one that ignores how difficult Reynolds could be, how selfish Wynette could be, and how racist the South was.

CAMP

The narrative in Nashville of Wynette's last years is of a talented artist falling off a substantial peak. This argument has merit — the singles dried up and the acclaim did too. She played smaller and smaller theaters. She didn't transition to film or television. The irony is that during this period she also had an international pop hit, made with a droll set of English pranksters. On 1991's "Justified and Ancient (Stand By the Jams),"[1] Wynette and the KLF are working in a camp mode — though this is a vexed term, as *camp* could be defined as the gap between what an artist is performing and what the artist thinks they're performing, often in concordance with an audience. This artifact, at the very end of her career, could have led to other possibilities. But this KLF collaboration was the last significant thing Wynette did before she died, and she died too young. It's possible to imagine another life for Wynette post KLF, one weirder and more open to other voices.

The KLF were art school clowns Jimmy Cauty and Bill Drummond, also known by the name, among other monikers, of the Justified Ancients of Mu Mu, or the Jams. They released cryptic ads in the music press, hired billboards no one could figure out. Their first number-one single, as the Timelords, was called "Doctorin' the Tardis," about the at-the-time deeply unfashionable TV series *Doctor Who*. They had a strongly meta quality, treating their performances as deeply political work about deeply unserious things. They wrote a book called *The Manual (How to Have a Number One the Easy Way)*, which worked well enough that they burned a million pounds as a joke. They were a pop band that cared as much about the French media conceptualist Guy Debord as they did about ABBA, and their resulting "underground gone massive" aesthetic brought the music of university clubs into stadiums.

The KLF's hit with Tammy Wynette came from a both/ and position. They were serious about her talent and skill, serious about bringing Nashville into England, and serious about the history of that practice; but also they were joking about the excesses of her taste, joking about the vastness of certain American pleasures, joking about US cultural domination. Wynette, in singing with the KLF, was being allowed to be in on the joke, to not be serious and thus to be deeply serious. Camp requires this kind of hyperawareness, an outsider methodology for worming one's way inside. At this moment in Wynette's career, she was on the outside.

The commercial appeal of "Justified and Ancient" can't be underestimated, especially its success on the pop chart, but like much of Wynette's life, even this is complicated. The chart expert and critic Chris Molanphy believes it sold well, but not well enough to get a gold record.[2] Though the music video was played often on MTV, video airplay wasn't counted toward gold status. The numbers are difficult to parse, but the best evidence I have suggests it sold about 200,000 copies altogether in the US and the UK. So there were both significant sales and significant airplay; however, just as significant is the fact that almost none of the radio play occurred on country stations.

"Stand By Your Man" makes for an interesting comparison. The song became a standard, with almost incalculable numbers. However, when it was released in 1968, things were a little different. Country radio goes through periods where there's a lot of pop crossover, which results in higher sales. In an email interview, Molanphy broke down the numbers for me. He pointed to the decade between the early 1950s and the early 1960s and the *Urban Cowboy* era of the early to mid-1980s as pop crossover periods. The year 1968 wasn't in one of those; in fact it was in a quite hermetic time for Nashville. Molanphy said of "Stand By Your Man" that "the fact that it never goes gold (at a time when gold meant a million in sales BTW) means it probably only did a couple hundred grand, total, during its run."[3]

He was referring to sales in the US and UK — and it went to number two in the UK. But it also did significant business in other countries. It was Wynette's first genuinely international breakthrough, hitting number one in eighteen countries. "Stand By Your Man," its closest equivalent in domestic (American) sales, did well in Canada, Australia, New Zealand, Belgium, and the Netherlands, but not nearly as well as the KLF song. "Stand By Your Man" hit number one in the UK, though.[4]

As with country music and drag, the KLF are made serious by an ability to take the piss out of themselves. "Justified and Ancient" is a mix of Malcolm McLaren–style white dub, Brixton hip hop, Pentecostal church-choir music, and Wynette's still-crystalline voice. The first words are from

Wynette, calling us to a place called Mu Mu Land, and the rest of the track works through exactly what or where Mu Mu Land might be.

This tour jives and explodes, moving into a mélange that reminds one of a po-faced, first-year art school remake of *Alice in Wonderland*. It takes place in that kind of space, one of both logical sense and dreamscape. The second half of the first verse has Wynette intoning,

> They called me up in Tennessee,
> They said "Tammy, stand by the Jams,"
> But if you don't like what they're going to do
> You better not stop them 'cause they're coming through.

The song is a history of what pop is and a schema of what pop could be — both of the cult and the ubiquitous. For example, "stand by the Jams" resembles "stand by your man" but also "kick out the jams," from the infamous MC5 track "Kick Out the Jams, Motherfucker."[5] Mashing up an anthem of extreme conservative domesticity with an anthem of personal and social liberation has a novel strangeness. "The Mu Mu" is a reference to an army that seeks to provide cosmic truth as a bulwark against conspiracy theories in the drug-fueled and mostly jokey *Illuminatus* series of sci-fi novels by Robert Anton Wilson. There is an aspect here of rescuing Wynette from the past, from the historical reality, and recognizing her as a kind of ancient diva.

What the first verse says seems to be what actually happened: they called up Tammy in Tennessee. In early summer of 1991, Cauty and Drummond were in a London studio trying to revive a song they had been kicking around since a fragment appeared on their 1987 debut album under the title "Hey Hey We Are Not the Monkees." Cauty wanted to replace the original singer and randomly suggested Wynette. Drummond, a fan not only of country but of Wynette, got on the phone and a week later was being picked up at the Nashville airport by none other than George Richey, "driving a powder blue Jag," McDonough quotes Drummond. Richey, recovering from open-heart surgery at the time, "sported 'snakeskin boots, fresh-pressed jeans, a wet-look perm.'" McDonough continues,

> Bill met his idol back at First Lady Acres as he stepped into the First Lady's pink beauty parlor. "Her fingers were being manicured by a young man as a woman teased her hair into some feathered concoction. Her free hand was flicking through the pages of *Vogue*." Tammy had a question for her new friend. "'Bill, you're from Scotland? Can you tell me why I have such a large lesbian following there?' I had no answer but promised to look into it."[6]

There is no mention of whether Drummond ever got back to Wynette about the lesbian fandom in Scotland. Drummond didn't ask how Wynette knew exactly the demographics of her fandom or their sexual identity.

I am genuinely confused by Wynette's taking this gig, but I love that she did. Maybe it was because she was bored, maybe because she was impressed by how these UK boys crossed the ocean to see her, maybe because she was curious, and maybe because she was game. Not only did she record this song, she appeared in the video as well.

The video has a collection of Club Kids types, the full Benetton rainbow, arrayed on something resembling a ziggurat. There is a Black woman in a tight silver dress and a Cleopatra wig and several other Black people singing, dancing, and beating drums; four Asian women in long blonde wigs and white robes; and six white people on another side of the ziggurat clad in canary-yellow silk. A control pad is imposed on the screen, with Wynette surrounded by graphic-design elements suggesting machinery. A chyron slides by explaining exactly who Wynette is in terms of the commercial success of "Stand By Your Man" and noting how many number-one singles she's had and how many gold records. Partly this is a reintroduction to the world, an explicit notice that even in this ironic tech utopia, even in the UK, Wynette is a legend who needs to be recognized. Wynette dances imperiously, wearing an azure gown with a long asure scarf and a very stylish crown.[7] It's arts-and-crafts camp, it uses ideas of the future to unsettle Wynette's authority, and it's making the very sincere, formalist argument that Wynette is not only the queen of country music but a cultural queen in general.

The song ended up being Wynette's last great commercial success. Since it was in part a novelty single, one might regret that she finished her career with a joke. But there's something refreshing about it as well. There was nothing at that point to indicate she would be dead within a few years.

The single and the video open a wide cluster of possible counterfactuals. Maybe Wynette would have had a new career in England; maybe she would have been rethought of as a kind of dance diva; maybe she would have had a renewed country music career. The strangeness of the video liberates critical thinking; it provides another venue for optimism. Maybe she could have been like Dusty Springfield, who was reclaimed in a similar way by the Pet Shop

Boys. Though Dusty was English, and queer, and the Pet Shops Boys were more arch and less weird than the KLF, Dusty's work with them resulted in sales and a reinvention of her career, as well as, perhaps, the re-canonization of *Dusty in Memphis*.

Wynette's question about Scottish lesbians as fans might have been a joke, but she did have queer fans. Her work with the KLF was an engagement, in its baroque and career-pleasing way, with an audience used to queer self-fashioning. Springfield and the Pet Shop Boys were mutually accustomed to that space, while the KLF and Tammy Wynette were using queer aesthetics but were not strictly queer themselves. There's a long legacy of gay men imprinting themselves on female stars in a tricky act of ownership, which might not be entirely in anyone's control.

One exception to this legacy is the funny southern burlesque *Sordid Lives*, a melodrama about a gay actor who comes back to small-town Texas for his grandmother's funeral. It began as a play and was adapted into a cult film in 2000,[8] then ran as a limited-run television show, followed by a sequel film in 2017 (with some diminishing returns). The movie features a group of southern actors who have written and acted in plays and television shows about the South, including Delta Burke, Rue McClanahan, and Leslie Jordan. Jordan plays a mama's boy who has spent the last twenty years dressing as Tammy Wynette. His performance is a rabid remixing of a drag queen's simultaneous desire to monstrously consume and critique a person they are a fan of, but also a difficult examination of what fandom can be — the desire not just to enjoy the music of a performer but to become the performer.

Not only does Jordan play Wynette through the whole enterprise, underlining the project's takedown-from-within of the South, but *Sordid Lives* features the same kind of loss, heartbreak, and especially concerns about domestic self-loathing and self-absorption that mark the best of Wynette's oeuvre. The domestic here features a literal homecoming. The movie is introduced by the grandson, in a therapist's office in West Hollywood, saying he's from the South, although he quickly distinguishes the South from Texas. He then talks about being raised a strict Southern Baptist, the denomination Wynette was raised in, a middle-of-the-road denomination deeply committed to gender roles as much as to a sense of social propriety.

The question the movie raises is how to be queer in the South, how to integrate desire into the expectations of southernness. Queerness here is a category of both sexuality and gender — the question could easily be amended to "how to be a sissy in the South." "Sissy" isn't a particularly southern category, but it has an edge in the South, a history, partially of resistance and partially of a conservative or reactionary understanding of gender. In being a woman or in being a sissy there is a kind of mutuality of suffering. To be a sissy isn't exactly to be a woman — femme is an expansive and all-consuming category — but to be a sissy is often to be treated like a woman.

This treatment includes violence. Men who beat women might justify it because the woman disobeyed, didn't toe the line. When a sissy is beaten, or forced into care, when their desires are "cured" by the church or the clinic, or when they're pushed away by their family, it's for similar reasons. It's because of a perceived refusal to acquiesce to the social order. "Sissy" as a category is a little old-fashioned to acknowledge as currently operational, but I think it still exists.

Being a sissy means not only being a mama's boy but also being interested in the roles motherhood plays—the material culture of mamahood. That is in itself a kind of key to southern womanhood. In interviews or in fan club newsletters, when Wynette brags about her ham or when there is conversation about her biscuits, she's performing that expectation of womanhood as much as when she's on stage. The kitchen is a public space in the South: learning to cook is like learning to sing, and learning how to organize a life, to keep a home clean, or make yourself and your family presentable—all are done with the expectation and desire for orderliness. The domestic is one of the spaces where the sissy and the mother intersect.

This overlap is often musical—the mama and the sissy bond over torch songs, lachrymose hymns, and domestic ballads. Singing through suffering makes it better, but I also think there is a certain kind of relief in the genderfucking that can occur when a femme man listens to songs of female suffering. There is something a little extra poignant when a man who has sex with men sings something like "Stand By Your Man." Of course, it can be a joke, the queer reversal of forms, the recognition of how *man* becomes a pliable object of desire, with a safe side and a dangerous side—the way the word *faggot* can be used as an intimate phrase of comradeship or as a sharp barb. But before gay marriage sublimated the queer cultures of sexual freedom and resistance to a straight-appearing, monogamous, bourgeois conventionality,[9] when someone in drag sang "Stand By Your Man," it encompassed a cruel joke about how a man can't be stood by in the conventional way, and the sadness that can occur when one wants a kind of devotion that seems impossible.

The worship of a diva is also the humiliation of the diva. When someone in a queer context sings something like "Stand By Your Man," they're interpreting the text, but they're also interpreting the performer. Such worship says to Wynette, "I can't have a man like the song tells me to have a man, but you sure couldn't either." Or even that under the prescribed circumstances of time and place, she spent a lot of time trying to be a woman but failed at being a woman. But with regard to drag, the success or failure of womanhood isn't the key. What's central is the slippage between real and false, between what is being performed and how it's being performed.

Sordid Lives is about a mainstream gay man figuring out how to be gay and having to go back to his Texan family (with whom he's closeted) for the funeral of a matriarch. The only out gay man in that environment is Brother Boy, played by Jordan. Brother Boy has been institutionalized for twenty-seven years for his flagrant cross-dressing.

There is some conversation about whether Brother Boy thinks he is Wynette and about whether his over-identification with the singer has prevented him from having a "normal" life, here defined as an exterior and interior life of heterosexuality. In a long, bizarre therapy session depicted in the film, made tender and difficult by Jordan, every possible way to be queer is elided and denied, even as the usual ways of being straight are being ignored. In the session, Jordan is made up and has earrings on, and has a Wynette wig in front of him. (The earrings look like they're from a Christmas album in the late 1970s; the hair comes from a bouffant style Wynette wore a decade before

that.) The therapist asks Brother Boy what he mastur-
bates to and tries to convince him to masturbate to images
of women. The therapist bullies him, calls him a failure,
mocks his inability to imagine women as part of his erotic
life, and eventually shows him her breasts and genitals.
There are moments where the performative camp of the
moment overwhelms, and moments where Jordan shows
how being Wynette or portraying Wynette is what makes
Brother Boy less lonely and happier. The scene ends with
him refusing to continue the sessions, refusing to be anything but Wynette. The performance becomes real, the
artifice allowing for a kind of authentic joy.

Brother Boy goes on to perform as Wynette in the insti-
tution's John Waters-esque rec room, in a bright orange
pantsuit, a bouffant wig, and more appropriate earrings.
He lip-syncs through "I Don't Wanna Play House," eventually interrupted by his cousin, who roars in and shoots
up the place with a silver six shooter. The cousin rescues
Brother Boy from the hospital through a back room, climb-
ing fences with him to make it just in time for their grandmother's funeral. Brother Boy slinks into that funeral in
a one-shoulder cocktail dress, black, slimming, and elegant — no longer Wynette but fully sissy, mourning and in
bloom, like something out of late Tennessee Williams.

Wynette as camp, Wynette as drag, Wynette as an unstable and insecure figure are all present here. It might seem
that Wynette is being made fun of in these texts — that the
KLF made fun of her or that Sordid Lives director Shores
made fun of her. There's a viral video separate from this
film, done in that ironic, highly juxtaposed, digital form,
in which every time Jordan comes on as Tammy Wynette
there's a cut to Wynette herself on television in the mid- to

late 1960s, in a bright orange, sequined pantsuit, singing on a fake front-porch stage set. The smash cuts deepen the meta quality, marking Wynette's own performance as drag and Jordan's as a tight reading of Wynette and of how we read and consider Wynette as an icon as much as we consider her as a performer or a figure from real life.

When queens perform Wynette, or the KLF puts Wynette in their song and video, or Jordan plays at being Wynette in a comedy, they're all working through a set of personas, a slippery double reversal. Partly it's about how women in Wynette's time and place existed, and how she performed her gender, with the kind of high material glamour of the South after World War II. Liberace dressed as he did partly as a way of proving to the world he was no longer poor. Parton dresses as she does partly for the same reason and also because she wants you to know that she knows the tits and the blonde hair are a performance. She wants to prove that she, in her high femmeness, can have a good time and still win against the men. These are acts of drag—if we define *drag* partly as being hyperaware of the performance of your own gender. The KLF hired Wynette because they thought she was doing drag in that way. Shores thought about hiring Wynette for his small domestic melodramas for similar reasons. Wynette knew how to put on womanhood. She did it every day—the near omnipresence of friend and hairdresser Jan Smith was part of that—but Wynette was so messy. Not messy in the fun, Leslie Jordan way, of high sissy as a way of fucking with the domestic. Not in the cruel way in which some drag acts mocked her. Wynette's messiness had a kind of overwhelming sadness.

People's domestic lives are unknowable, and people's

interior lives are rarely made exterior. We depend, especially with celebrities, on how people appear in public. The wet-look perm and snakeskin boots Richey wears in Drummond's depiction of his visit to Nashville, that great diva image of the nails being done while she flips through an issue of *Vogue* — that's Tammy Wynette doing performance for her English guests. That's being glamorous and seamless, even at home, in order to get a gig. She wasn't messy there.

FUNERAL

Tammy Wynette died on April 6, 1998, in front of the TV, on a small couch, in a small condo. She had gone from shack to apartment to tract house to mansion to country estate to Nashville mansion to downsized condo, packed with garish rugs, overstuffed couches, kitschy pencil drawings of country music stars, and more Lucite than seems reasonable.

There is some controversy about exactly what happened. When Richey described the time immediately preceding it to Gerry Wood, a journalist and intimate of the couple's, he claimed,

> I had been up for two days and nights because Tammy had a very tough weekend. During the day, we were napping on the couch in the kitchen. I recall hearing Tammy say several times to the housekeeper, "Please be quiet. Try to let him rest. He's had very little rest this weekend—he's been up with me."[1]

Even in death, Wynette's narratives were gnarled. What is central here, as with the kidnapping, as with the domestic scandals, is an unsolvable ambivalence. The reader can never fully know how Wynette lived or even how she died.

Richey said he went down for a nap and when he got up, there was a note from the housekeeper, Cleta Ramsey, saying she had run to the store. He continued,

> When I came out of the bathroom and sat down where I had been napping, I looked over at Tammy, and I thought, I'm not too sure she's breathing! I moved over next to her and felt her foot. . . . Her legs were cold from the knees down. I immediately made a telephone call to her doctor, Wallis Marsh, in Pittsburgh.[2]

Richey said he called the doctor at 7:01, which means Wynette died between 6 and 7 p.m.

Jan Smith said she received a call from someone at half past five who said that Wynette had died. Another friend of Wynette's said she received a call at about six that gave her the same information. Richey claimed that he alone had discovered Wynette's death, but the police report says it was both Richey and Ramsey who found the body. Ramsey has never given an interview about the death. Mark Crawford, the groundskeeper for the condo building, said he had accompanied Ramsey to the store, but he became "agitated" when asked to discuss exactly what time he saw Wynette that evening, and whether she was alive or dead. McDonough states that Wynette's daughter Gwen was told sometime after seven, and she let her sisters Tina and Jackie know, but that Tammy's other daughter, Georgette, at the time working as a nurse, had to be told by one of her coworkers, who learned it from TV.[3]

In the two hours between 6:55 (the latest that Wynette could have died, according to Richey) and 8:55 p.m., no one called 911. Richey claimed to have called the family doctor, but others questioned that. Much later, the family lawyer, Ralph Gordon, called non-emergency authorities. (Wynette often mixed business and pleasure. Gordon regularly did legal work for her and Richey, but on that day, according to McDonough's reporting, he was acting only as a friend.) Wynette's body was eventually moved, at 2:30 a.m., to Woodlawn Mortuary. In the time between 9:00 p.m. and 2:30 a.m., any pain medications that Wynette had in the house were swept away.[4] Her cause of death was initially recorded as a pulmonary embolism.

As with the kidnapping, we know the start point and the end point, but what happened in between is unclear. Wynette had friends around her, and she had close relationships with her friends, but she was fodder for both tabloid and legitimate media. This doesn't add clarity but means that people with competing social and financial interests, sometimes even friends, told different stories, depending on need or convenience. The same person could have told different stories to the police, the family, and the media. At least one person, an employee at the medical examiner's office, may have sold part of the story to the *Globe* later.[5] Even in death, Wynette's central narrative was the absence of one.

Wynette lived and died in the tabloids. She sued the *Star* and the *National Enquirer* in 1997 after a nurse leaked her medical records to them.[6] Animosity toward the tabloids was part of a long pattern — though she went to *People* or *Cosmopolitan* herself when she needed to talk to the media, the tabloids were always interested in her. When she went from the hospital to the Betty Ford Center in 1986, Leo Katz reported on it for the *Enquirer*.[7] As discussed earlier, right before she married Michael Tomlin, a story about her dating Burt Reynolds was about to be on the front page of the same newspaper.[8] And her autobiography was excerpted in a 1979 edition of the *Star*.[9]

The *National Enquirer* was among the first sources to report on Wynette's death and the financial improprieties that followed it. Its reporting was heavily detailed and featured competing, unnamed sources. Wynette's daughter Jackie Daly thought the sources came from Richey's camp, and there were rumors that Richey's friends, or maybe even Richey himself, called in tips.[10] The *Enquirer*'s base readership had a class overlap with country music fandom, and the paper's stories about country scandals often helped keep it afloat. The tabloid traded in both social and financial capital. It's as if Daly and her functionaries were talking to Richey and his functionaries via competing editorial copy in the most popular tabloid in America.

The melodramatic, almost true-crime aspect of the end of Wynette's life was tabloid material as a formalist gesture — both in the supermarket periodicals but also in how her family wrote about her. Daly's memoir emphasizes the vagueness of the events leading up to her mother's death, mostly as an argument that Richey was responsible for them; her account functions as some combination of a jeremiad against a stepfather, an attempt to explain arcane legal language, and a keen record of the loss of a parent. Daly didn't think Richey deliberately killed Wynette but that he was reckless with her health, in particular contributing to her addiction to pain medications and failing to take her to the hospital when she needed care. It's less about the daily life of Wynette and more about her long shadow. There was a similar shape to the questions of where the money was and where the medications were when Wynette died, and asking who was responsible for that death mirrors the same questions about addiction, familial connections, and capital that marked her life.[11]

Daly's concerns about Richey had some merit. The lawsuits around the estate took almost four years to wrap up—three of Wynette's daughters sued Richey over his care of their mother, and Wallis Marsh for malpractice in overprescribing drugs, prescribing the wrong drugs, and not following up properly.[12] From the press coverage and from their memoirs, it seems as though Wynette's children cared about her but did not know how best to care *for* her. Richey's handling of the couple's finances when Wynette died is less clear. The daughters argued with Wynette's last husband about where their mother's money went, but there are possibilities other than misconduct. Married couples share finances, and it might be reasonable to assume Wynette supported Richey willingly because she liked his company. Wynette was sick for a long time, and she was frail for a long time. Her health was on a continual decline, partly due to her likely continued addiction to prescription opiates. She was also in a lot of pain, living with the ongoing consequences of a hard life. Long, lingering deaths, with the amount of medical care that Wynette underwent, are expensive.

Wynette spent the last six years of her life in and out of hospitals. She went through a number of surgeries, including a hysterectomy. She was often in and out of consciousness. Her last decade was a gradual collapse. She died in her sleep in the early evening, with her husband gone to the bathroom. Her friends and her lawyer were nearby, but not there. That group of people had been through a long, macabre wait for the inevitable.

An assessment of the decades of ill health is central to understanding Wynette's late career. In one of the most poignant sections of Daly's book about her mother, she talks about the last time Wynette performed at the Grand Ole Opry, on May 17, 1997, eleven months before her death. She notes that a family friend there, Phyllis Hill, who worked for the Nashville Network for fifteen years, commented on how frail and thin Wynette was and how much trouble she had with the performance:

> This was a woman nearly in tears, nervous, distraught, unable to keep her earrings on or to button her clothes properly. Various attendants were buzzing around her, adjusting and primping her, but they couldn't make the adjustments she really needed. They couldn't tame the beast that was eating at her insides.[13]

Daly's memoir positions Wynette as a virtuous hero destroying herself to bring country music to her loyal fans and Richey as a villain feeding her pills to keep her working and alienating her children.

The basic facts are accurate, and they certainly are jarring: that Tammy Wynette gave a performance at the Grand Ole Opry in her final year, that she was in pain during that performance, that she had trouble dressing herself, or standing upright, and despite all of that, she performed anyway.[14] We know she had dressers, and we can safely assume that even if Richey hadn't been there that night, he might have had some influence in getting her on that stage. Daly quotes Hill again as saying, "If I was Richey I would stop her from going on," and then tells of Richey ushering Wynette off the stage at the end of the performance, straight to the bus, and preventing anyone from seeing her — the clear implication being that Richey was both forcing her to perform and isolating her from people who might think it was a bad idea.[15]

But what happens if we recast the anecdote, treating Wynette as an autonomous agent? She performed when she was in pain because she had been performing for most of her adult life, and she never really turned a gig down. She had pride in her work ethic. Wynette performed when she was in pain because Wynette was never *not* in pain. As Burt Reynolds had said when her people called to say she was sick and wouldn't be able to work on *Evening Shade* in two weeks, "I know her, she'll be up singing. . . . I mean, you'd have to shoot her right between the eyes, and *then*, she'd still finish 'Stand By Your Man.'"[16] She performed at the Opry that night because she needed the money, or because she needed the adulation of fans, or because, in some way, the Opry would always be home to her. And maybe she was a little bit lonely. It's possible she chose to support Richey because, as someone on the edges of the music business, he understood that her relationship with her audience gave his wife purpose.

This Daly anecdote concludes a section about wills, estates, and meetings. Her mother's funeral gets only one line. A public memorial for Wynette took place at Ryman Auditorium on Thursday, April 9, 1998, a few hours after a more private event was held within view of the Ryman. The public memorial service was broadcast live on CNN.[17]

The service was a combination of appearances by old country legends, neotraditionalists, and people who were up and coming in the 1990s. It excluded much of new Nashville and was a surprisingly compact 110 minutes. There was a preshow, consisting of interviews with people going into the funeral—catch-as-catch-can moments. Some of the Oak Ridge Boys talked about listening to Wynette on the radio, all the way to Philly or New Jersey. The rest of the interviews suggest two almost contradictory readings of her career: that she was a universalist loved by everyone or that she was, in the words of Jean Shepard, "the last great female traditionalist country stylist." The emphasis there being on *female*. Gene Weed, an Academy of Country Music Awards producer, said before the service, in an awkward moment, that Wynette's life work consisted of ladies' songs designed for ladies. (Though it seemed that Weed wasn't quite sure what a ladies' song was, or how it differed in design.)

Listening to the public eulogies, a viewer gets the impression that no one ever really knew Wynette. The memorial had an undertone of trying to figure out exactly who Wynette was. Ambivalence is never a good tone for a funeral, and the places where ambivalence punctured the expected reverent atmosphere made everyone a little uncomfortable. CNN interspersed archival interviews throughout, including a 1989 interview with Larry King during which King mostly babbles but accidentally gets a good quote now and then—for example, Wynette surprisingly says that she didn't have an act or even a personality until she married George Jones and performed with him.

The pastor James Murray, from a church that Wynette didn't really attend, delivered a generic short sermon, not giving the listener much succor, but he did mention real estate: the nice house that Wynette had in Franklin, and the nicer house that she now had in heaven. The fact that Wynette was struggling with finances at the time of her death made the mention of real estate especially awkward.

The performances that followed, with few exceptions, were blandly Baptist, centering on nineteenth-century hymns, often accompanied by somewhat off-kilter stories. You had the band J. D. Sumner and the Stamps, three elderly men fronted by a much younger new recruit, singing a decently harmonized version of "Peace in the Valley," and "Angel Band," which tended toward restraint, no speaking in tongues, no trills, no extended runs. Randy Travis followed with a not-perfect if slightly preserved-in-amber version of "Precious Memories." Rudy Gatlin told us that Wynette liked to clap on the one and the three, and that they were playing in G because A was too fast, before sliding into a slick rendition of "I'll Fly Away." It was one of the few moments when Wynette's musicianship was mentioned. Lorrie Morgan did a very subtle, very low-key, meditative version of "Amazing Grace," without a lot of theatrics. The productions were as slick and as studio-ready as Wynette's work, smart in their way, melding tradition and new production.

Loretta Lynn was absent, too grief-stricken to attend, and this was mentioned by the pastor, by the Oak Ridge Boys, and by Dolly Parton. But it makes one think about who else was missing: Rodney Crowell, Willie Nelson, and Kris Kristofferson, for instance, of the Austin crowd. Linda Ronstadt. Of the up and comers, Garth Brooks, Martina McBride, Pam Tillis, and K. T. Oslin. Wynette's cohort could have performed but didn't: Connie Smith, June Carter Cash, Jan Howard (Jean Shepard was there but didn't perform). Even some genuine outsiders could have played. The KLF would never have been invited to play the Ryman, but Elvis Costello was close to Jones and had played the Ryman. He could have delivered something strange and new.

That said, it might partly have been a question of the short time frame. In a tribute album released a few months after Wynette's death, some of these corrections were made. The album includes a resigned Melissa Etheridge recording of "Apartment #9," a fantastic performance of "Stand By Your Man" from the newly sober Elton John, a wry feminist retelling of "Your Good Girl's Gonna Go Bad" by K. T. Oslin, and the deep harmonies of Harris, Ronstadt, and Anna and Kate McGarrigle on "Golden Ring."[18] That it included Etheridge and John makes it one of the memorials that didn't ignore Wynette's queer fans.

Even at the Ryman that night, there were exceptions, a few performers who told stories that were as genuine or as queer or as weird as the tribute CD, including the Judds, the inestimable Parton, and a slightly unhinged Merle Haggard, who sent a video for the service. Naomi Judd talked about meeting Wynette at an industry schmooze fest for some DJs in Nashville, and how Wynette introduced herself and they had a conversation about what to do with kids while on tour. Judd noted how ordinary the conversation was in the midst of calling Wynette an "archetypal queen." This move between diva and mother, between arch performer and ordinary domestic, was the dialectic that marked Wynette's life. Judd quoted Wynette as saying, "You're gonna miss birthday parties and proms, and they're gonna get mad at you, but you'll be able to put her through college and give her a lifestyle." The weight of that difference between a life and a lifestyle was made even more poignant by the fact that Wynonna, Judd's daughter, was there at the service and soon joined her mother on stage. Naomi Judd also said that just as Wynette had always maintained her beautician's license, Judd still had her nursing license, a reminder of economic anxiety and of the fact that performance, motherhood, nursing, and being a beautician are all types of high femme labor. When Wynonna came out, clad in a plain, floor-length, butch duster, unadorned, she gave a performance of "How Great Thou Art" that was subversively closer to Jones's early rockabilly than to Wynette's honky-tonk sorrow.

The most significant and haunting appearance was Parton's. Knowing that she was the biggest star there, but also that it wasn't her show, Parton came across at her most charming, sweet, and low key. Her speech could not have been extemporaneous—Parton is too careful for that—but it sounded like it. She explained that her and Wynette's fellow honky-tonk angel, Lynn, wasn't there because she was too broken up to make it. The absence of her friends Wynette, by death, and Lynn, for emotional reasons, prioritized Parton's star power and functioned as a marker of a kind of shift: that with Wynette's death, a kind of country singing went with her. Though Lynn was still alive, Parton was now the first lady of country music, in a reign over another kind of music, another territory, and another understanding of home (one that is less domestically fraught).

Parton made sure that the memorial service was about Wynette, subtly avoiding complex Nashville politics and thus demonstrating old-school southern manners, in the best sense of the word. This could be seen in how she spoke of a time in 1992 when Wynette had sought her help with makeup and hair while she was in the hospital. This was a reminder that Wynette had been in and out of the hospital for at least six years—to her inner circle, her death couldn't have been a surprise.

Parton talked about power in other ways. She said that Richey encouraged her to tell this ribald story at the public service: She said that when they were both starting out, Wynette asked her what to do about how it looked to go on the road with Porter Wagoner. Parton, rolling up to the punch line in a soft, sly way, said she told her friend, "Oh Tammy, you surely can't worry about stuff like that. First of all, half the people wouldn't believe it, and the other half would just think we had bad taste."

Parton has learned to make bad taste a joke — she knows people will think of her as not having had proper raising and leans into it in the best way she knows how. Wynette, I think, had anxiety about being in poor taste, as Parton's memory showed and perhaps was meant to show, not unkindly but wisely. Worrying about bad taste, about your reputation, about what other people think of you, might just be lethal.

Parton then sang a chorus of a song she and Tammy had begun writing together, called "Didn't Hear the Thunder," a fragmented note of inspiration, followed by a new song of hers, "Shine On." This new song, outside of the traditional hymnal, was a final gift to Wynette, treating her as someone still capable of sparking new work. Parton's whole presentation showed a discreet generosity, offering the gift of her labor to a woman who died in anxiety over her own cultural relevance. Parton said Wynette "shined then, she's shinin' now, and she'll shine forevermore." She closed her appearance with the final chorus of "I Will Always Love You," a song whose definition of love once again proved to be expansive.

If Parton provided a master class in how to perform at a funeral, Merle Haggard's performance was on the opposite end of the spectrum.

Haggard was recorded somewhere in California. He seemed not very aware of his surroundings. He didn't frame the shot well. He was on a piano bench, with a photo of him and Wynette behind him, but the screen was filled by his face. He referred to "George" in an ambivalent way, making me realize that throughout the proceedings I often didn't know whether a speaker who mentioned "George" was talking about Richey or Jones. Haggard's confusion placed the rest of the memorial's confusion in context. He said it was impossible for him to be there, which made me wonder why, and why he was the only one of the no-shows to send in a recording. (No doubt some of them were on the road — an appropriate tribute to Wynette's memory, in a way, to miss an important family obligation due to being on the road.)

Haggard looked rough as he started singing "If I Could Only Fly" — the only one, aside from Parton, to sing something from his canon instead of the traditional hymnody. He was off-key, mumbling every so often, and he never explained exactly why he was singing this song. He didn't tell a story about Wynette or otherwise indicate who he was in relation to her. They must have known each other, must have sung with each other — in a sense they were linked by becoming iconic for having songs that were deeply politically misunderstood ("Stand By Your Man" for Tammy, "Okie from Muskogee" for Merle).

Haggard had performed "If I Could Only Fly," written by Blaze Foley, before the service, but he didn't record it until the early aughts. When performing the song for the memorial, a year after he had last sung it at a friend's funeral, he is awkward. Haggard's work here pushes a kind of failed ambition. At the end of his video, in one of the most poignant moments of the memorial, Haggard said,

"That's the best I could do. It's not very good, but good-bye, Tammy." He was right about the performance, but I wonder if we also can say that about how Nashville treated Wynette in general: not very good.

When he took the stage, George Richey, the last of Wynette's string of not-good-enough husbands, looking exhausted and frail, in a few words thanked Sherrill, Jones, and other industry people before he mentioned the kids and grandkids — reminding us that this was still an industry event regardless of how many of the fellow performers talked about Wynette as a mother. Wynette may have been country music's foremost mother, as Maybelle Carter was in her day — and maybe being a symbolic mother is easier than being a real mother. However, it was in service of an idea of motherhood that rewarded suffering. Wynette as mother of a genre, and as mother of actual children, suffered in extravagantly sentimental ways, and the funeral was her last significant show.

CONCLUSION

I wrote this in my fortieth year. I have never had a long-term partner, or, frankly, a short-term partner. I have lived in four cities in the last twenty years and in those cities in more than forty places. When I was in school, I did sometimes live in dorms, but mostly I lived in rooms in houses with strangers. I find it hard to cook or clean. I do not have children. There are centuries of people like me, rootless urban cosmopolitans. Conservatives have always had opinions about people like us — that because we purportedly have no roots, we are destroying families out of revenge; that we don't understand the so-called traditional family, and therefore we seek to destroy it.

Part of the conservative discourse is anti-Semitic, and part of it is homophobic. I am not a Jew, but I am very queer.

It's true that I did spend some of my twenties not knowing anyone with kids, spending my money on pleasure, and thinking that my roots were loose. I spent some time thinking about the intersections between family and state. In my angrier moments, I believed strongly in both smashing the family and smashing the state. I had close friends, though, and I always maintain that friendships are as worthy as any relationship. One of the ways I thought about rebuilding all of that smashing was via friendship.

My friends have children now, and I am spending time with them and their families — observing their birthdays, eating at their tables, holding their babies, telling stories. I have stable housing, and sometimes (though not in the middle of a pandemic) those friends and their babies come over to visit with me. I make sure they get toys on birthdays, eggnog at Christmas, candy at Easter and Halloween. I am less willing now to "smash" the delicate, difficult lives of people I love.

I think, though, still, that when a man and a woman marry, and they have children, they go into a room and close the door. No one can know exactly what happens in the domestic lives of other people. Even the best writers of the domestic write about what happens when the whole business collapses, or is made public. Wynette's best work is about when the most private failures become public scandals. There is less consideration of the quotidian details of other people's lives, in the basic grind, without scandal, without public disclosure. Not knowing about Wynette is more common than assuming we can know anything.

I have spent the bulk of this book not talking about myself and trying to talk about Wynette. I have read the major biographies, but often they are about her husbands and her children (who wrote some of them) more than they are about her. They are less about her work than they are about the repeated collapse of her domestic life. This book has been me trying to figure out her work, her talent, and her skills, and to take that work seriously. However, Wynette's work largely was about the domestic, so that meant talking about relationships that confuse me, that isolate me, and that I find hostile — even if I have surrounded myself with people who love me and include me in their domestic lives.

I have been thinking about this for a long time. In my senior year of high school the teacher gave us an assignment where we had to analyze country music lyrics. She had a list of funny titles and funny lines. It was the first time I had experience with the joke being taken seriously. I presented on Tammy Wynette and "Stand By Your Man." I had a lot of thoughts: that Hillary Clinton wasn't fair with her comment, that it was a difficult song, that it would never be my life, that I loved it, and that it was as exotic, as untranslatable, as the Gilberto Gil I had discovered the previous summer. I don't think Wynette has ever not been exotic for me, and I also don't think my decades-long opinion that she was treated badly will ever change. She needs to be seriously considered.

This serious consideration for me deepened in 2014 or 2015. I posted on Facebook about why Wynette was being lost compared to the rest of her cohort. There was a certain amount of discussion, and then I put the idea out of my head. It returned to me in Seattle, where I go every spring to be with a collection of academics and critics who think seriously about country music of all types. To be honest, for a lot of people in my life, outside of my music critics' coterie, my interest in country music is an eccentricity at best, and at worst a betrayal of all the work I have done trying to escape my small-town upbringing, of this adult life I have made for myself in Toronto or Montreal.

At the tail end of a half-sober conversation after a long night, a night full of the job talk that is common among critics — sort of arguments but not really arguments — we landed on Wynette. On why she was out of the mix, why she wasn't either considered like Parton or reclaimed like Lynn. I was also in a moment of my life where I was reconsidering my priorities. I had moved to another city, to another social scene, and my friends were having babies or had already had babies. The women had husbands; the husbands had wives; they took monogamy seriously and many of them were religious. Before my move to Hamilton, Ontario, the only time I had really been with kids was when I had spent two weeks one fall in suburban Chicago with a church musician who had the conventional children and wife and property scenario. Because we spent time at the Art Institute, ate at interesting restaurants, and he played difficult music, I didn't think about it, but those Chicago times gave me permission to love other children, other families.

I thought then a lot about what it meant to have children, what it meant to own property, about what heartbreak meant in a context that was largely normative but was under-considered, at least in my imaginary. I started making work explicitly about this novelty — a photo series of me holding my new friends' babies, essays about Sam Hunt and suburban Atlanta. My mom, whose life goals tended toward the suburban stability that I had abandoned, got sick, and I wrote essays about hymns, Protestant mourning, and the desire for this kind of stability.

I thought a lot about what popular music was and what popularity meant. Wynette was important to me at this moment because she provided a way of thinking through what this kind of domesticity meant. A few years later, when Trump won, it made me reconsider the moral consequences of this kind of reactionary moment. I thought about how I could be in love with a singer like Wynette when I knew what her politics were, like the often-ignored capitalism of Parton, like the explicit Trump support of Lynn. How could I love this kind of music when this kind of music was pushing an agenda that would severely compromise my life?

I thought about David Cantwell and Bill Friskics-Warren's book *Heartaches by the Number* and how they named Sammi Smith's "Help Me Make It through the Night" as their best country song of all time.[1] I kept arguing with cishet white men of a certain kind about the saddest country song of all time, and I kept moving toward Wynette. I am convinced that performance is authorship and that Wynette's "Apartment #9" is the saddest song ever written (though I will take notes for "I Don't Wanna Play House" or "D-I-V-O-R-C-E"). Tammy Wynette matters as a great singer, as a great constructor of odes to the domestic, as a political figure, as a woman who has not been given credit. When I talk about "Apartment #9" being the saddest song ever written, I want to extend that argument. Though I never want to tell other people what country is, for me, the heartbreak songs are the songs that break apart houses, more than the ones that talk about ramblers and rounders. I want to prove that every straight white boy who talks about how "The Grand Tour" is the saddest song of all time has not seriously considered the above fact. Also, the best George Jones songs are secretly Tammy Wynette songs in drag. I am talking about, of course, "He Stopped Loving Her Today."

When Jones sings "He Stopped Loving Her Today," it's easier to think about a dead wife than a live one. Critics often allow Jones's talent and skill to hide how difficult he was to Wynette, how he was abusive, verbally, and how he threatened her, and maybe even hit her. When we say Tammy Wynette matters, it's another kind of feminism, one that takes seriously the depiction of women's work, in ways that Jones or fans of Jones haven't.

It's also feminist in other ways. Sometimes people talk about Tammy Wynette only in context with Billy Sherrill or George Jones. McDonough did this too. The concentration on Sherrill suggests that a man is responsible for Wynette's success, that even smart critics are bad at figuring out how the intricate relationships between the performer, the producer, and the writer work in Nashville. Wynette is one of the great interpretive singers in American popular music, as good in her way and in her genre as Sarah Vaughan, but we don't consider honky-tonk singers as interpretive singers.

I think the quality of interpretation and the nature of what is being interpreted are also key here. There is something significant about how Wynette turned the stories of her life into myth—about the ambivalence of exactly how much work she did in the cotton fields, about that story of the beautician's license that was trotted out at every turn, about how she shed her husbands when they were no longer useful and how she made the messy, ugly breakups into something gorgeous and alive. I think it matters how we make lives. I also think that with queer lives and women's lives, so much is assumed to be confessional, every story is thought to be reportage, every song or work of art is assumed to come from those acts of reportage like objective truth. Instead we can look at how memoir can be crafted into something mythic, and how that mythic crafting functions as one source among many, one kind of drafting of memory into fiction. The grift of the autobiography, the stardom of a well-constructed riff on that mythologized autobiography, I think that matters because it resists that smaller autobiographical impulse.

There's an old joke by the radio comedian Ed Gardner about scratching the tinsel of Hollywood to find the real tinsel underneath, and I don't think that's only true about Hollywood.[2] Maybe it's truer with Nashville, where everything has to be authentic, but where there is danger both in being too authentic and in someone figuring out you have a schtick. Being too authentic, as we define it, being too traditional, perhaps forgetting the crafting of a persona, means that one is stuck in a previous version of oneself that an audience might view as old-fashioned or limited by tradition. But reinvent yourself too much and the novelty becomes grating and is not seen as checking off complex genre boxes. I think trying to figure out what authenticity means, how it is constructed, matters. This is made even more complex by gender. Because of misogyny, people think women's personas are automatically either not crafted or they are too crafted. This is how Tammy Wynette got trapped.

That we think of her as a "tragic country queen," yet she made autonomous choices, this one is the hardest for me. I think part of her persona was that of a good worker and a good mother. (Since Parton is childless she has avoided some of the misogyny found in the pressure to be both.) Wynette had four children. The tell-alls by two of her kids that appeared after her death were largely about her death, with postmortem questions about the cause of death. They are not like Linda Sexton writing about the abuse she suffered under her mother, the confessional poet Anne Sexton; or Christina Crawford's lurid depictions of beatings at the hands of Joan Crawford.

I think she had a traumatic childhood, and I think she made bad choices about men, but they were her choices to make. I think that if we are going to talk seriously about sexual ethics in our culture, we need to start thinking about how, in her case, her choices were made, and not that she was in the middle of a great love story (the men she married were abusive) but that she divorced these men yet continued the pattern with the next one. I think that considering why someone matters involves investigating their bad choices, bad patterns, and weighing them within a social context. Wynette was a woman, but she was also a resting place for a wide variety of contradictory stories we tell ourselves as a culture. We know the stories about where she is miserable, but we don't know the stories where she is happy. That includes all the time she spent in the 1970s with Burt Reynolds, the Zelig of American redneck pleasure.

She knew what her reputation was, and she knew what people said about her. Her commitment to a persona was a commitment to a kind of public performance. She was smart about how she constructed herself, but being in on the joke and smart about the joke meant that she did morally corrupt things. She performed at rallies for George Wallace. Like Phyllis Schlafly, she took advantage of the benefits brought about by the women's movement while arguing for a "traditional" femininity. She didn't speak out about Vietnam. She let dumb and mean people use her work against her. She took a lot of money from morally compromised people, and when it was politically convenient for her, she pushed back, but only a little.

We need to stop thinking that performing gender is something that liberals do as an act of moral good. We like to think of Loretta Lynn as the singer of "Rated X," but we don't like to think that she voted for Trump. Tammy Wynette matters because how she used high femme armor against other women is still current practice.

Even if Wynette's politics were terrible, even if her relationships were vexed, she got fucked over. The men in her life made money off of her, for example, and male critics still talk more about Jones or Sherrill in her life than about her lifelong friendship with the hairdresser Jan Smith or the complex give and take between her, Lynn, and Parton. That she is underplayed and not really written about, compared to Lynn and Parton, shows her skills and talents have slipped under the radar of public consciousness. Her dozens of hits have been subsumed by the colossal misreading of "Stand By Your Man," so much so that people treat her like a one-hit wonder.

When the inevitable critical revival of Wynette happens, I want to be there to make sure that her whole life isn't forgotten. That her complex and difficult life does not go unexamined, that a full moral inventory happens and then we sit down and agree that "Apartment #9" is still the saddest country song ever sung.

On a more personal level, as a nonbinary artist and critic who is deeply committed to Wynette as a performer and a writer, the idea of putting on your womanhood has a tender resonance. There is a subversive, queer potential to knowing that drag can come in all feelings, that the hard, longing melancholy for a lover that Wynette posits here can also be the longing for a performative gender that functions, that allows her desires to be absorbed.

That said, I see the compulsory heterosexuality of Wynette. I do not understand having babies, I do not understand the pain and exhaustion of balancing the domestic and a full career. I don't know how people make those choices. I want to know how the domestic works. Country music's consideration of the domestic is done in the context of an audience of people who belong to it, and so those who are outside its sphere are not allowed to be external critics of it. Partly this is because working-class gender and sexuality are vastly under-considered, partly this is because I rarely share my domestic life with anyone, and partly this is because I grew up where country music taught us that the domestic is paramount (though more of a Martina McBride, Mary Chapin Carpenter kind of thing). I think Wynette matters to me because I want to know how straight people live, how their rituals are constructed, and how their lives take shape. I know we are in the middle of this post-gender, post-sexuality moment where none of this really matters and gender or sex is a free-floating miasma, but people who from where Wynette is from still take it very seriously.

Tammy Wynette matters to me, because taking her seriously is a way of taking the domestic seriously, refusing to dismiss those narratives, to recognize their artistic and social importance. As a trans and queer person, I don't want to give Wynette over to the transphobes and the homophobes, because I think that mutually trying to understand cultural signs allows for a larger and more complex political reading, and because I want my privilege to be known.

ACKNOWLEDGMENTS

I am grateful for:

Susan Easton, the first person who taught me how to read a text and to love country music.

Ben R, Carl, Casey, Cim, Kim, and Kyler, who were careful readers and editors.

Gloria, for her brilliant and rigorous copyediting and her generous suggestions; the book would have been much shabbier without her.

Debra Kelly, who assigned me "Stand By Your Man" in grade twelve.

Aaron, who displayed endless patience and profound ethical care in working through so many of these ideas.

Al, Alissa, Ashley, Ben N, Brandon, Brittani, Cath, Charles, Danica, Dave W, Gareth, Griffin, Jacqueline, James, Jamie, Josh M, JP, Matt, Nate J, Nate W, Rob, Robyn, Scott, Sonali, and Tara, for making the city of Hamilton a safe place to land.

Col, D, Glenys, Pat, and Ray, for being my oldest friends.

Graham, Harley, Lucas, Mack, Mari, and Renato, who are keeping the politics of the West translatable years after I moved east.

David P, in autistic solidarity.

Alfred, Amanda, Ann, Charles H, David C, Francesca, Jewly, Jody R, Joey, Marissa, Nadine, Stuart H, and Thomas I, for keeping the potential of music criticism alive and kicking.

Josh L, for his tenderness and his skill as a musician and for introducing me to the erotic potential of Kenosha, especially Woodman's.

Kristy H, Martin, and Travis, for continually believing in a queer critical renewal.

And especially, especially for:

Adelaide, Xavier, Benedict, James, Louis, Georgia, Sam, Juniper, Evie, Caleb, Aubri, Malcolm, Alex, Morgan, Annika, Riley, Sarah, Marcel, Lyra, Zach, Rhett, Harrison, Gwendolyn, Finn, Deacon, and all my friends' kids, for allowing me to access the domestic, a space I had always found isolating and unfriendly.

In the current cultural climate, where transphobia and homophobia are frothing themselves into a moral panic, writing a book that foregrounds a nonbinary and queer reading of a heterosexist space would be angrier and less nuanced without access to your homes and lives.

A portion of the royalties from this book will go to trans-friendly nonprofits in Texas to combat recent legislative violence.

NOTES

Introduction

1. Carrie Horton, "Every CMA Awards Male and Female Vocalist of the Year Winner Ever."
2. Claire Wilson, "Tammy Wynette."
3. "Wynette Autopsy Finds Heart Failure Cause of Death."
4. Tammy Wynette, *Stand By Your Man: An Autobiography*, with Joan Dew, 159–160, 169; Jackie Daly, *Tammy Wynette: A Daughter Recalls Her Mother's Tragic Life and Death*, with Tom Carter, 139; Georgette Jones, *The Three of Us: Growing Up with Tammy and George*, with Patsi Bale Cox, 112; Kristin McMurran and Dolly Carlisle, "A Battered Tammy Wynette Relives the Macabre Abduction That Nearly Killed Her"; Eve Zibart, "Tammy on a Tightrope"; Annie Zaleski, "Forty-three Years Ago: Tammy Wynette Reportedly Abducted in Nashville."
5. Tammy Wynette, "Apartment #9," by Johnny Paycheck, Fern Foley (Bobby Austin), and Fuzzy Owen, Epic, 1966, 7" vinyl recording; later released on Wynette's debut studio album, *Your Good Girl's Gonna Go Bad*, track 1, Epic, 1967, vinyl recording.
6. Bobby Austin, "Apartment #9," by Johnny Paycheck, Fern Foley (Bobby Austin), and Fuzzy Owen, track 1 on *Apartment #9*, Capitol, 1967, vinyl recording.
7. Jimmy McDonough, *Tammy Wynette: Tragic Country Queen*, 122.
8. Tyler Mahan Coe, "Being Together: The George Jones and Tammy Wynette Story"; "Country Singers Join Wallace's Son at Rally"; Peter La Chapelle, *I'd Fight the World: A Political History of Old-Time, Hillbilly, and Country Music*, 220; Peter La Chapelle, "A Visual Thread about the Decades of Support the Country Music Industry and #Opry Members Gave to the Nation's Most Famous Segregationist, George C. Wallace."
9. Wynette, *Stand By Your Man*, 159–160, 169; Nick Tosches, "The Devil in George Jones."
10. McDonough, *Tammy Wynette*, 18–25.
11. McDonough pulled his punches. His biography of Wynette is dotted with fictionalized versions of events — things he wanted to say to Wynette, and things he wanted to include as part of the discourse but that he might have had trouble citing. In one of those passages, he says, "So now we get to the kidnapping, for the first time the world doesn't believe you.

Changed everything, didn't it?" (*Tammy Wynette*, 264). McDonough here speaks for himself (he didn't believe her), then moves on to discussing the matter from other angles. Coe notes the differences in details about the harassment and vandalism at Wynette's home between Joan Dew's 1977 profile of Wynette in *Singers and Sweethearts: The Women of Country Music* (14–62) and the singer's own explanation in her 1979 autobiography *Stand By Your Man* (written with Dew), saying Dew believed Wynette might have picked up some notes from *One Flew Over the Cuckoo's Nest*, Ken Kesey's 1962 novel that was made into a movie in 1975. Tyler Mahan Coe, "Loved It Away: Tammy Wynette, On Her Own."

12. Wynette sued the *Enquirer* (and the *Star*) near the end of her life for invasion of privacy and defamation of character. "Tammy vs. Tabloids."

Domesticity

1. McDonough was helpful here.
2. Tammy Wynette, "I Don't Wanna Play House," by Billy Sherrill and Glenn Sutton, track 1 on *Take Me to Your World / I Don't Wanna Play House*, Epic, 1968, vinyl recording.
3. Loretta Lynn, *Fist City*, Decca, 1968, vinyl recording.
4. Joel Whitburn, *The* Billboard *Book of Top 40 Country Hits*, 395–397.
5. "Tammy Wynette, Artist," Grammy Awards; "Stand By Your Man," Grammy Hall of Fame.
6. Patricia Brake Howard, "Tennessee in War and Peace: The Impact of World War II on State Economic Trends."
7. McDonough, *Tammy Wynette*, 19–20.
8. McDonough, *Tammy Wynette*, 20.
9. Jennifer Justus, "Country Cooking: Minnie's Corn Pudding and Tammy's Better Than Sex Cake"; McDonough, *Tammy Wynette*, 361–362.
10. McDonough, *Tammy Wynette*, 21, 41–46.
11. Tyler Mahan Coe, "Loneliness Surrounds: Virginia Wynette Pugh."
12. Roy Clark, "I Never Picked Cotton," by Bobby George and Charles Williams, track 4 on *I Never Picked Cotton*, Dot, 1970, vinyl recording.
13. McDonough points this out (*Tammy Wynette*, 43), but also, one of the last images of Wynette, shot by Harry Langdon for Epic Records, circa 1995, features the bowl prominently.

High Femme Armor

1. Wynette, *Stand By Your Man*, 102.
2. Wynette, *Stand By Your Man*, 63–66; McDonough, *Tammy Wynette*, 100–101.

3. Wynette, *Stand By Your Man*, 322.
4. Wynette, *Stand By Your Man*, 9, 11.
5. "Tammy Wynette Bio."
6. Samantha Drake, "The Story behind Tammy Wynette's Tragic Life."
7. Miles Corwin, "Tammy Wynette: First Lady of Country."
8. Jim Presnell, "Country Music Brings Special Luster to Fair."
9. McDonough, *Tammy Wynette*, 7.
10. Jones, *The Three of Us*, 107.
11. Dolly Parton, quoted in Lauren Collins, "Looking Swell."
12. "Memorial for Tammy Wynette." Dolly Parton told about doing this for her friend at the public memorial service.
13. Tammy Wynette, "Satin Sheets," by John E. Volinkaty, track 5 on *Another Lonely Song*, Epic, 1974, vinyl recording.
14. *The Bill Anderson Show*, 1967, available at https://www.youtube.com /watch?v=o8H0C9HrZNY.
15. *The Wilburn Brothers Show*, "Tammy Wynette"; "Tammy Wynette — Final Opry Appearance (With Lorrie Morgan)," video.
16. Dolly told this joke on Jimmy Fallon's show in 2016, among many other times. *The Tonight Show Starring Jimmy Fallon*, August 4, 2016, NBC.
17. Alanna Nash, *Behind Closed Doors: Talking with the Legends of Country Music*, 236.
18. Erin Duvall, quoted in Kelly Brickey, "Author Erin Duvall Dishes on New Book, *Country Music Hair*."
19. George W. S. Trow, "Two Musical Gatherings."
20. Tammy Wynette, "Your Good Girl's Gonna Go Bad," by Billy Sherrill and Glenn Sutton, track 6 on *Your Good Girl's Gonna Go Bad*, Epic, 1967, vinyl recording.

Soft Politics

1. Tammy Wynette, "Stand By Your Man," by Billy Sherrill and Tammy Wynette, track 1 on *Stand By Your Man*, Epic, 1969, vinyl recording.
2. Marc Myers, "The Love Song of Virginia Pugh"; Anita Bugg, "Stand By Your Man."
3. Evelyn Shriver, quoted in Bugg, "Stand By Your Man."
4. McDonough, *Tammy Wynette*, 156; Bugg, "Stand By Your Man"; Cary O'Dell, "'Stand By Your Man' — Tammy Wynette (1968)."
5. Wynette, *Stand By Your Man*, 189.
6. Bugg, "Stand By Your Man"; Myers, "Love Song."
7. Eleanor Clift, "Songs of Non-Liberation."
8. Billy Sherrill, quoted in Myers, "Love Song," and Bugg, "Stand By Your Man."

9. Tammy Wynette, "Run, Woman, Run," by Ann Booth, Duke Goff, and Dan Hoffman, track 1 on *The First Lady*, Epic, 1970, vinyl recording; RCA Records, advertisement, *Billboard*, August 29, 1970, 39.

10. Hank Williams, "I'm So Lonesome I Could Cry," by Hank Williams and Paul Giley, track 4 on *Moanin' the Blue*, MGM, 1952, vinyl recording.

11. Wynette, *Stand By Your Man*, 190.

12. Betty Friedan, *The Feminine Mystique*, 294.

13. Wynette, *Stand By Your Man*, 194.

14. Parton's husband's name is Carl Dean; he worked in transportation for a while. Sarah Smarsh devotes a paragraph to him in her book on Parton, *She Come By It Natural: Dolly Parton and the Women Who Lived Her Songs*, 69.

15. Loretta Lynn, *Still Woman Enough: A Memoir*, written with Patsi Bale Cox, xiv.

16. This is too short a space to rework the political legacy of Wallace, but it's foregrounded by his January 14, 1963, speech, in which he committed to "segregation now, segregation tomorrow and segregation forever." See "'Segregation Forever': A Fiery Pledge Forgiven, but Not Forgotten."

17. La Chapelle, *I'd Fight the World*, 219–231, esp. 219, 230, 231.

18. For the best-sourced discussion of Donham's lie being responsible for Till's death, see Timothy B. Tyson, *The Blood of Emmett Till*.

19. Whitburn, *The* Billboard *Book*, 395–397.

20. Billy Sherrill, quoted in Bugg, "Stand By Your Man."

21. Dolly Parton, in Jad Abumrad, "Sad Ass Songs." Katie Herzog, in "Dolly Parton Is Not a Feminist," does a significant unpacking of the implications of this.

22. Me First and the Gimme Gimmes, "Stand By Your Man," by Tammy Wynette and Billy Sherrill, track 8 on *Blow in the Wind*, Fat Wreck Chords, 2001, CD.

23. Lyle Lovett, "Stand By Your Man," by Tammy Wynette and Billy Sherrill, track 8 on *Lyle Lovett and His Large Band*, MCA, 1989, CD. During a Q and A as part of a talk in the International Association for the Study of Popular Music's Popular Music Books in Process Series (https://www.iaspm.net/popular-music-books-in-process-series/), Gus Stadler noted the prevalence of both the original song and Lovett's cover in the gay bars of his young adulthood.

24. Hillary Clinton, in Bill Clinton and Hillary Clinton interview by Steve Kroft.

Pain

1. Daughter Jackie Daly's memoir, *Tammy Wynette: A Daughter Recalls Her Mother's Tragic Life and Death*, is unusually transparent about Wynette's late addiction and health crises.
2. Wynette, *Stand By Your Man*, 63-65; McDonough, *Tammy Wynette*, 50, discussing an interview Wynette gave to the *Star* tabloid in 1998.
3. Wynette, *Stand By Your Man*, 116.
4. McDonough, *Tammy Wynette*, 103; Wynette, *Stand By Your Man*, 71; Daly, *Tammy Wynette*, 70.
5. Spacek starred as Lynn in Apted's film *Coal Miner's Daughter*; Wynette's TV movie was *Stand By Your Man*, a 1981 biopic directed by Jerry Jameson.
6. McDonough, *Tammy Wynette*, 145.
7. Wynette, *Stand By Your Man*, 159-160, 169; Tosches, "The Devil in George Jones."
8. Loretta Lynn, *Coal Miner's Daughter*, with George Vecsey, 123, 174; Lynn, *Still Woman Enough*, xiv, 120.
9. Wynette, *Stand By Your Man*, 292-301, 331.
10. Joan Dew, "Queen of Country Music."
11. Daly, *Tammy Wynette*, 149-151.
12. Daly, *Tammy Wynette*, 192-202.
13. Coe, "Loved It Away." Coe's podcast/website is usually immaculately sourced, but he doesn't specify his sources here. Georgette Jones tells about the fire and vandalism of their home in the Fox News story "Georgette Jones: Mother Tammy Wynette Plagued with Problems, Kidnapping Threats."
14. Daly, *Tammy Wynette*, 149-151.
15. McDonough, *Tammy Wynette*, 173-175.
16. The shopping was less of a cause than being caught in the middle of the savings and loan scandal of the 1980s. She would eventually have to declare bankruptcy, in 1988. See "Country Music Singer Files for Bankruptcy."
17. With the possible exception of *Rhinestone*, the movies Parton made between 1980 and 1989 were significant box office successes and in the case of *9 to 5* and *Steel Magnolias* also had some critical success.
18. Sissy Spacek won an Academy Award for her portrayal of Lynn in *Coal Miner's Daughter*.
19. Mary A. Bufwack and Robert K. Oermann, *Finding Her Voice: The Saga of Women in Country Music*, 335.
20. Daly, *Tammy Wynette*, 102.

21. Reba McEntire, "Tammy Wynette Kind of Pain," by Brandy Clark, Mark Narmore, and Shelley Skidmore, track 4 on *Stronger than the Truth*, Rockin' R, 2019, CD.

22. Mary A. Bufwack, "Tammy Wynette."

23. Kellie Pickler, "Where's Tammy Wynette?," by Don Poythress, Jimmy Ritchey, and Leslie Satcher, track 1 on *100 Proof*, BNA, XIX Recordings, 2011, CD.

24. Waylon Jennings, "Are You Sure Hank Done It This Way," by Waylon Jennings, track 1 on *Dreaming My Dreams*, RCA Victor, 1975, vinyl recording.

25. "Spade Cooley Indicted in Murder of His Wife."

26. Richard Ben Cramer, "The Strange and Mysterious Death of Mrs. Jerry Lee Lewis."

27. Edward Morris, "Stay Apart and Shut Up, Judge Tells Lorrie and Sammy." Again, this might have been drinking and fighting as much as it was direct abuse, but Morgan's luck with husbands was as bad as Wynette's.

28. The Cagle case is complicated. Both he and his partner, Jennifer Tant, were arrested for domestic violence, but Tant refused to testify against Cagle and he was found not guilty. "Chris Cagle, Girlfriend Jailed on Domestic Assault Charges"; Gayle Thompson, "Chris Cagle Not Guilty in Domestic Violence Charge."

29. In *I Saw the Light: The Biography of Hank Williams*, Colin Escott states that Williams died of a weakened heart helped along by "alcohol, chloral hydrate, and morphine," 272.

30. Peter Guralnick's *Careless Love: The Unmaking of Elvis Presley* reports that Presley's autopsy noted fourteen drugs in his body at the time of death.

31. See Terry Jennings, *Waylon*, for a discussion of pills as well.

32. Chelsea J. Carter, "The Long, Tortured Journey of Mindy McCready."

33. Nick Tosches, *Country: The Twisted Roots of Rock 'n' Roll*; Tosches, "The Devil in George Jones."

Melodrama

1. McMurran and Carlisle, "A Battered Tammy Wynette"; Zibart, "Tammy on a Tightrope."

2. Daly, *Tammy Wynette*, 133–137; Jones, *The Three of Us*, 118.

3. McMurran and Carlisle, "A Battered Tammy Wynette."

4. McMurran and Carlisle, "A Battered Tammy Wynette"; Zaleski, "Forty-three Years Ago"; Daly, *Tammy Wynette*, 139; Jones, *The Three of Us*, 112.

5. McDonough, *Tammy Wynette*, 247–251; Daly, *Tammy Wynette*, 129–135; Jones, *The Three of Us*, 117–119.

6. McDonough, *Tammy Wynette*, 415; Jones, *The Three of Us*, 210; Daly, *Tammy Wynette*, 111.

7. Coe, "Loved It Away"; McMurran and Carlisle, "A Battered Tammy Wynette"; Zaleski, "Forty-three Years Ago"; Daly, *Tammy Wynette*, 97-98; McDonough, *Tammy Wynette*, 429. Coe and Daly both do a good rundown of the opinions of men that Wynette was somehow to blame for the harassment.

8. McMurran and Carlisle, "A Battered Tammy Wynette"; McDonough, *Tammy Wynette*, 245.

9. Daly, *Tammy Wynette*, 129-135 (quotes on 132); *Autopsy: The Last Hours of . . .*, "Tammy Wynette" (Daly interview); McMurran and Carlisle, "A Battered Tammy Wynette."

10. Daly, *Tammy Wynette*, 133.

11. Named after the album *Wanted! The Outlaws* (RCA). Released in late 1976, the compilation with Willie Nelson, Waylon Jennings, Jessi Colter, and Tompall Glaser sold well enough to name the movement that had been underway for a few years. The title is a bit of a misnomer, as the record is still, in its way, studio slick.

12. Whitburn, *The* Billboard *Book*, 395-397.

13. An argument that reminds me of John Waters's 2000 movie *Cecil B. Demented*.

14. George Jones, "The Grand Tour," by Norro Wilson, George Richey, and Carmol Taylor, track 1 on *The Grand Tour*, Epic, 1974, vinyl recording.

15. McDonough, *Tammy Wynette*, 247.

16. Daly, in *Autopsy: The Last Hours of . . .*, "Tammy Wynette."

17. Daly, *Tammy Wynette*, 101.

18. Wynette, *Stand By Your Man*, 195-196; McDonough, *Tammy Wynette*, 378. Jones himself denied it in his 1996 autobiography *I Lived to Tell It All*, with Tom Carter, 229-230.

19. McDonough, *Tammy Wynette*, 379.

20. McMurran and Carlisle, "A Battered Tammy Wynette."

21. McMurran and Carlisle, "A Battered Tammy Wynette."

22. Daly, *Tammy Wynette*, 133; Jones, *The Three of Us*, 112.

23. Wynette, *Stand By Your Man*, 71; McDonough, *Tammy Wynette*, 103; Daly, *Tammy Wynette*, 70.

24. Sarah H. Lisanby, Jill H. Maddox, Joan Prudic, D. P. Devanand, and Harold A. Sackheim, "The Effects of Electroconvulsive Therapy on Memory of Autobiographical and Public Events."

25. Alanna Nash, quoted in McDonough, *Tammy Wynette*, 249.

Sex

1. Tammy Wynette, *Womanhood*, Epic, 1978, vinyl recording.
2. Willie Nelson, *Phases and Stages*, Atlantic, 1974, vinyl recording.
3. Bob Dylan, *Blood on the Tracks*, Columbia, 1975, vinyl recording.
4. N.C., review of *Womanhood*, by Tammy Wynette.
5. Willie Nelson, *Stardust*, Columbia, 1978, vinyl recording.
6. Tammy Wynette, "Womanhood," by Bobby Braddock, track 1 on *Womanhood*, Epic, 1978, vinyl recording.
7. Tammy Wynette, "D-I-V-O-R-C-E," by Bobby Braddock and Curly Putman, track 7 on *D-I-V-O-R-C-E*, Epic, 1968, vinyl recording.
8. Bobby Braddock, *Bobby Braddock: A Life on Nashville's Music Row*, 152.
9. "Nashville Edition."
10. "The Sexes: Total Fascination." The book was written in 1963, and by the mid-1970s, hundreds of thousands of people were taking classes on the topic.
11. Tammy Wynette, "You Oughta Hear the Song," by Roger Bowling and Jody Emerson, track 3 on *Womanhood*, Epic, 1978, vinyl recording.
12. Tammy Wynette, "The One Song I Never Could Write," by Wayland Holyfield, track 5 on *Womanhood*, Epic, 1978, vinyl recording.
13. Tammy Wynette, "I'd Like to See Jesus (On the Midnight Special)," by Robert Seay and Dorval Lynn Smith, track 6 on *Womanhood*, Epic, 1978, vinyl recording.

Fame

1. George Jones and Tammy Wynette, *We Go Together*, Epic, 1971, vinyl recording.
2. George Jones and Tammy Wynette, *Me and the First Lady*, Epic, 1972, vinyl recording.
3. George Jones and Tammy Wynette, *Let's Build a World Together*, Epic, 1973, vinyl recording.
4. George Jones and Tammy Wynette, *George and Tammy and Tina*, Epic, 1975, vinyl recording.
5. George Jones and Tammy Wynette, *Golden Ring*, Epic, 1976, vinyl recording.
6. Joel Whitburn, *Hot Country Songs 1944 to 2008*, 215. The Discogs entries for these albums are quite thorough: see "George Jones and Tammy Wynette Discography."
7. Tosches, "The Devil in George Jones"; Jones, *I Lived to Tell It All*, 309. Coe makes the point about this autobiography that Carter did all the research, wrote the book, and then brought it to Jones, who simply

confirmed. However, because at that point Jones's memory was shot after a lifetime of drugs and alcohol, the text is unreliable at best. Tyler Mahan Coe, "Season 2 Library."

8. Coe, "Being Together"; Wynette, *Stand By Your Man*, 159–160, 169. Coe was helpful here.

9. George Jones and Tammy Wynette, *We're Gonna Hold On*, Epic, 1973, vinyl recording.

10. George Jones and Tammy Wynette, "Roll in My Sweet Baby's Arms."

11. George Jones and Tammy Wynette, "Two Story House," by David H. Lindsey, Douglas Glenn Tubb, and Tammy Wynette, track 6 on *Together Again*, Epic, 1980, vinyl recording.

12. *Sesame Street*, "Johnny Cash Visits."

13. Johnny Cash, "The Chicken in Black," by Gary Gentry, CBS, 1984, 7" vinyl recording; later on *A Boy Named Sue and Other Story Songs*, track 10, Sony, 2001, CD.

14. Tammy Wynette and George Jones, "(We're Not) The Jet Set," by Bobby Braddock, track 6 on *We're Gonna Hold On*, Epic, 1973, vinyl recording.

15. Charles Hughes was helpful with some of the concise rewording in this passage.

16. Whitburn, *The* Billboard *Book*, 433.

17. Richard A. Peterson, "Class Unconsciousness in Country Music," 57.

18. Merle Haggard, "Okie from Muskogee," by Merle Haggard and Eddie Burris, track 20 on *Okie from Muskogee*, Capitol, 1969, vinyl recording. David Cantwell's biography of Merle Haggard, *The Running Kind: Listening to Merle Haggard*, is necessary reading, not only about the Hag but for the context of race and class in this era.

19. Robbie Fulks and Jodee Lewis, "(We're Not) The Jet Set."

20. Waylon Jennings, "Luckenbach, Texas," by Bobby Emmons and Chips Moman, track 1 on *Ol' Waylon*, RCA, 1977, vinyl recording.

21. Loretta Lynn, "One's on the Way," by Shel Silverstein, track 1 on *One's on the Way*, Decca, 1972, vinyl recording.

22. Richard Goldstein, "My Country Music Problem—and Yours," 114. That Goldstein, a *Village Voice* writer, wrote this for urban, sophisticated women in a fashion magazine like *Mademoiselle* instead of for the more working- or middle-class audiences of *McCall's* or *Redbook* is worth noting.

23. John Prine, "Unwed Fathers," by John Prine and Bobby Braddock, track 10 on *Aimless Love*, Oh Boy, 1984, CD; Wynette, "Unwed Fathers," by Prine and Braddock, track 1 on *Even the Strong Get Lonely*, Epic, 1983, vinyl recording.

24. John Prine, "Paradise," by John Prine, track 5 on *John Prine*, Atlantic, 1973, vinyl recording.

25. John Prine and Iris DeMent, "(We're Not) The Jet Set," by Bobby Braddock, track 1 on *In Spite of Ourselves*, Oh Boy, 1999, CD.

Tradition

1. The liner notes for this trio's reissues are unclear on this. In my conversations with other historians and country music critics, I learned that there might have been recording sessions in 1976—there definitely were conversations, rehearsals, and appearances on other people's media properties that year, and there were more formal sessions in 1978. Charles Hughes, Barry Shank, Martin Kavka, and David Cantwell, correspondence with author. See "Sisters in Country: Dolly, Linda and Emmylou."
2. *Dolly*, "Featuring Emmylou Harris and Linda Ronstadt."
3. Liner notes, *Trio: The Complete Trio Collection* box set (Rhino, 2016); liner notes, Emmylou Harris rarities collection *Songbird: Rare Tracks and Forbidden Gems* (Rhino, 2007); Stephen Padgett, "Years in the Making, *Trio* Comes Together."
4. Dolly Parton, Loretta Lynn, and Tammy Wynette, *Honky Tonk Angels*, Columbia, 1993, CD.
5. McDonough, *Tammy Wynette*, 317.
6. Dolly Parton, Loretta Lynn, and Tammy Wynette, "Silver Threads and Golden Needles," by Dick Reynolds and Jack Rhodes, track 3 on *Honky Tonk Angels*, Columbia, 1993, CD.
7. Walter C. Miller, dir., *Twenty-seventh Annual Country Music Association Awards*.
8. Dolly Parton, Loretta Lynn, and Tammy Wynette, "Silver Threads and Golden Needles," video.

Reprieve

1. John Boorman, dir., *Deliverance*.
2. Burt Reynolds, *Ask Me What I Am*, Mercury/Phonogram, 1973, vinyl recording. See Courtney Fox, "Inside Burt Reynolds' Forgotten 1973 Country Album *Ask Me What I Am*."
3. McDonough, *Tammy Wynette*, 253.
4. Jennifer Sangalang, "Burt Reynolds and His Many Ties to Florida"; John Maines, "Burt Reynolds' Gigantic Estate Will Become Million-Dollar Homes."
5. "Country Music Singer Files for Bankruptcy."
6. Joe Edwards, "A Full Life, but Wynette's Not Through Yet."
7. "Tammy Wynette: The 'Tragic Country Queen.'"
8. McDonough, *Tammy Wynette*, 435–437.

9. Wynette, *Stand By Your Man*, 270.
10. Coe, "Loved It Away." It's also worth noting how much of Wynette's depiction of the relationship is mediated by the *Enquirer*; see Wynette, *Stand By Your Man*, 263–280.
11. Colin Higgins, dir., *The Best Little Whorehouse in Texas*.
12. Sally Field, *In Pieces: A Memoir*, 235.
13. See Coe, "Loved It Away," and Wynette, *Stand By Your Man*, 263–280.
14. Merle Haggard, "Big City," by Merle Haggard and Dean Holloway, track 1 on *Big City*, Epic, 1981, vinyl recording.
15. "Tammy Wynette: Burt Reynolds Theatre (Jupiter, FL)."
16. *Evening Shade*, "The Fabulous Frazier Girls."
17. Tammy Wynette, in Burt Reynolds and Tammy Wynette, interview (Evening Shade/Country Music).
18. Hillary Clinton, in Clinton and Clinton, interview.
19. McDonough, *Tammy Wynette*, 341, 347.

Camp

1. The KLF and Tammy Wynette, "Justified and Ancient (Stand By the Jams)," by Jimmy Cauty and Bill Drummond, track 9 on *The White Room*, Liberation, 1991, CD.
2. Chris Molanphy, email message to author, April 2022.
3. Molanphy, email message.
4. Molanphy, email message.
5. MC5, "Kick Out the Jams, Motherfucker," track 2 on *Kick Out the Jams*, Elektra, 1969, vinyl recording.
6. McDonough, *Tammy Wynette*, 308.
7. The KLF, "Justified and Ancient," video.
8. Del Shores, dir., *Sordid Lives*.
9. Yasmin Nair has been necessary in her critique of gay marriage. Yasmin Nair, "On Kink at Pride."

Funeral

1. George Richey, quoted in Gerry Wood, *Tales from Country Music*, with Paul Zamek, 141.
2. Richey, quoted in Wood, *Tales from Country Music*, 141–142.
3. McDonough, *Tammy Wynette*, 344.
4. McDonough, *Tammy Wynette*, 351.
5. "Wynette's Death Questioned."
6. "Tammy Wynette Sues Supermarket Tabloids."
7. Leo Katz, *National Enquirer*, November 3, 1986.

8. Wynette, *Stand By Your Man*, 270.
9. Daly, *Tammy Wynette*, 217.
10. Daly, *Tammy Wynette*, 227–228.
11. Daly, *Tammy Wynette*, 212–217.
12. "Wynette Autopsy." Richey was dropped from these lawsuits after the exhumation of Wynette's body in 1999 and a determination that the cause of death was heart failure; like everything else about Wynette's life, the details about other possible causes were murky.
13. Phyllis Hill, quoted in Daly, *Tammy Wynette*, 208.
14. McDonough, *Tammy Wynette*, 337; "Tammy Wynette — Final Opry Appearance (With Lorrie Morgan)," video. The performance itself looks fairly high energy, but Wynette masked well.
15. Daly, *Tammy Wynette*, 208.
16. Reynolds, in Reynolds and Wynette, interview.
17. "Memorial for Tammy Wynette."
18. Various Artists, *Tammy Wynette Remembered*, Asylum, 1998, CD.

Conclusion

1. David Cantwell and Bill Friskics-Warren, *Heartaches by the Number: Country Music's 500 Greatest Singles*, 1–2.
2. Hedda Hopper, in "Looking at Hollywood," one of her Hedda Hopper's Hollywood columns, credits this joke to Gardner. It's also been attributed to Oscar Levant, Henry Morgan, and others.

BIBLIOGRAPHY

Abumrad, Jad. "Sad Ass Songs." October 15, 2019. *Dolly Parton's America.*
    Podcast. Produced by Shima Oliaee and WNYC Studios. New York Public
    Radio. https://www.wnycstudios.org/podcasts/dolly-partons-america
    /episodes/sad-ass-songs.
Autopsy: The Last Hours of . . . Season 4, episode 1, "Tammy Wynette." 2015,
    Reelz.
Boorman, John, dir. *Deliverance.* Elmer Enterprises, 1972.
Braddock, Bobby. *Bobby Braddock: A Life on Nashville's Music Row.* Nashville:
    Country Music Foundation Press, 2015.
Brickey, Kelly. "Author Erin Duvall Dishes on New Book, *Country Music
    Hair.*" Sounds Like Nashville. November 28, 2016. https://www
    .soundslikenashville.com/fashion-design/author-erin-duvall-dishes-on
    -new-book-country-music-hair/.
Bufwack, Mary A. "Tammy Wynette." Member bio, Country Music Hall of
    Fame. Accessed June 30, 2022. https://countrymusichalloffame.org/artist
    /tammy-wynette/.
Bufwack, Mary A., and Robert K. Oermann. *Finding Her Voice: The Saga of
    Women in Country Music.* New York: Crown, 1993.
Bugg, Anita. "Stand By Your Man." *All Things Considered*, NPR, October 28,
    2000. https://www.npr.org/2000/10/28/1113153/tammy-wynettes-stand
    -by-your-man.
Cantwell, David. *The Running Kind: Listening to Merle Haggard.* Austin:
    University of Texas Press, rev. ed., 2022.
Cantwell, David, and Bill Friskics-Warren. *Heartaches by the Number: Country
    Music's 500 Greatest Singles.* Nashville: Vanderbilt University Press, 2003.
Carter, Chelsea J. "The Long, Tortured Journey of Mindy McCready." CNN,
    Entertainment. February 18, 2013. https://www.cnn.com/2013/02/18
    /showbiz/ent-mindy-mccready-timeline.
Cauty, Jimmy, and Bill Drummond. *The Manual (How to Have a Number One
    the Easy Way).* London: KLF Publications, 1988.
"Chris Cagle, Girlfriend Jailed on Domestic Assault Charges." CMT News.
    May 28, 2008. http://www.cmt.com/news/1588143/chris-cagle-girlfriend
    -jailed-on-domestic-assault-charges/.
Clift, Eleanor. "Songs of Non-Liberation." *Newsweek*, August 2, 1971.
Clinton, Bill, and Hillary Clinton. Interview by Steve Kroft. *60 Minutes*,
    January 26, 1992, CBS.

Coe, Tyler Mahan. "Being Together: The George Jones and Tammy Wynette Story." Season 2, episode CR025/PH11. November 9, 2021. *Cocaine and Rhinestones*. Podcast. https://cocaineandrhinestones.com/george-jones -tammy-wynette.

Coe, Tyler Mahan. "Loneliness Surrounds: Virginia Wynette Pugh." Season 2, episode CR023/PH09. August 10, 2021. *Cocaine and Rhinestones*. Podcast. https://cocaineandrhinestones.com/virginia-wynette-pugh.

Coe, Tyler Mahan. "Loved It Away: Tammy Wynette, On Her Own." Season 2, episode CR026/PH12. November 23, 2021. *Cocaine and Rhinestones*. Podcast. https://cocaineandrhinestones.com/tammy-wynette.

Coe, Tyler Mahan. "Season 2 Library." *Cocaine and Rhinestones*. Podcast. https://cocaineandrhinestones.com/season-2-library.

Collins, Lauren. "Looking Swell." *New Yorker*, April 27, 2009. https://www .newyorker.com/magazine/2009/05/04/looking-swell.

Corwin, Miles. "Tammy Wynette: First Lady of Country." *Los Angeles Times*, April 7, 1998. https://www.latimes.com/archives/la-xpm-1998-apr-07-mn -36971-story.html.

"Country Music Singer Files for Bankruptcy." UPI, September 21, 1988. https://www.upi.com/Archives/1988/09/21/Country-music-singer-files -for-bankruptcy/8842590817600/.

"Country Singers Join Wallace's Son at Rally." *New York Times*, June 12, 1972, L32. https://www.nytimes.com/1972/06/12/archives/country-singers -join-wallaces-son-at-rally.html.

Cramer, Richard Ben. "The Strange and Mysterious Death of Mrs. Jerry Lee Lewis." *Rolling Stone*, March 1, 1984. https://www.rollingstone.com /culture/culture-features/the-strange-and-mysterious-death-of-mrs -jerry-lee-lewis-179980/.

Daly, Jackie F. *Tammy Wynette: A Daughter Recalls Her Mother's Tragic Life and Death*. With Tom Carter. New York: Putnam, 2000.

Dew, Joan. "Queen of Country Music." *Cosmopolitan*, April 1978.

Dew, Joan. *Singers and Sweethearts: The Women of Country Music*. New York: Doubleday, 1977.

Dolly. Season 1, episode 6, "Featuring Emmylou Harris and Linda Ronstadt." October 18, 1976. Available at https://www.youtube.com/watch?v= 3fbxHgum498.

Drake, Samantha. "The Story behind Tammy Wynette's Tragic Life." *Country Living*, September 15, 2017. https://www.countryliving.com/life /entertainment/a44810/tragic-life-of-tammy-wynette/.

Duvall, Erin. *Country Music Hair*. New York: HarperCollins, 2016.

Edwards, Joe. "A Full Life, but Wynette's Not Through Yet." *Greensboro News and Record*, October 17, 1991; updated January 28, 2015. https://greensboro

.com/a-full-life-but-wynettes-not-through-yet/article_2f7e3a2e-b8b9
-534d-96e3-e144b02ef1b4.html.

Escott, Colin. *I Saw the Light: The Biography of Hank Williams*. With George
Merritt and William MacEwen. New York: Back Bay Books, 2004.

Evening Shade. Season 4, episode 19, "The Fabulous Frazier Girls." Mozark
Productions. February 28, 1994, CBS.

Field, Sally. *In Pieces: A Memoir*. New York: Grand Central, 2018.

Fox, Courtney. "Inside Burt Reynolds' Forgotten 1973 Country Album *Ask
Me What I Am*." Wide Open Country. March 9, 2020. https://www
.wideopencountry.com/burt-reynolds-album.

Friedan, Betty. *The Feminine Mystique*. New York: Norton, 1963.

Fulks, Robbie, and Jodee Lewis. "(We're Not) The Jet Set." Live performance,
The Hideout, Chicago, July 8, 2013. Hmc1410, YouTube, July 14, 2013.
https://www.youtube.com/watch?v=3FhYYrU2orQ.

"George Jones and Tammy Wynette Discography." Discogs. Accessed January
24, 2022. https://www.discogs.com/artist/1993987-George-Jones-Tammy
-Wynette.

"Georgette Jones: Mother Tammy Wynette Plagued with Problems,
Kidnapping Threats." Fox News. April 26, 2018. https://www.foxnews
.com/entertainment/georgette-jones-mother-tammy-wynette-plagued
-with-problems-kidnapping-threats.

Goldstein, Richard. "My Country Music Problem—and Yours." *Mademoiselle*,
June 1973.

Guralnick, Peter. *Careless Love: The Unmaking of Elvis Presley*. New York:
Back Bay, 2000.

Herzog, Katie. "Dolly Parton Is Not a Feminist." *The Stranger*, November 22,
2019. https://www.thestranger.com/slog/2019/11/22/42064346/dolly
-parton-is-not-a-feminist.

Higgins, Colin, dir. *The Best Little Whorehouse in Texas*. Miller-Milkis-Boyett,
RKO, 1982.

Hopper, Hedda. "Looking at Hollywood." Hedda Hopper's Hollywood, *Los
Angeles Times*, November 27, 1947, A10.

Horton, Carrie. "Every CMA Awards Male and Female Vocalist of the Year
Winner Ever." The Boot. November 8, 2021. https://theboot.com/cma
-awards-male-vocalist-of-the-year-female-vocalist-of-the-year-winners/.

Howard, Patricia Brake. "Tennessee in War and Peace: The Impact of World
War II on State Economic Trends." *Tennessee Historical Quarterly* 51, no. 1
(1992): 51–71. http://www.jstor.org/stable/42626986.

Jameson, Jerry, dir. *Stand By Your Man*. May 13, 1981, CBS.

Jennings, Terry. *Waylon*. New York: Hachette, 2017.

Jones, George. *I Lived to Tell It All*. With Tom Carter. New York: Villard, 1996.

Jones, George, and Tammy Wynette. "Roll in My Sweet Baby's Arms." Live performance, Wembley Stadium, London, April 1981. Makeminecountry2, YouTube, August 25, 2008. https://www.youtube.com/watch?v=bYJjq _o97Ms.

Jones, Georgette. *The Three of Us: Growing Up with Tammy and George*. With Patsi Bale Cox. New York: Atria, 2013.

Justus, Jennifer. "Country Cooking: Minnie's Corn Pudding and Tammy's Better than Sex Cake." The Bitter Southerner. https://bittersoutherner .com/cooking-country-women-food-nashville.

The KLF. "Justified and Ancient." Video, directed by Bill Butt. An Atlas Adventure, KLF Communications. KLF, YouTube, December 31, 2020. https://www.youtube.com/watch?v=XP5oHL3zBDg.

La Chapelle, Peter. "A Visual Thread about the Decades of Support the Country Music Industry and #Opry Members Gave to the Nation's Most Famous Segregationist, George C. Wallace." Thread Reader. June 13, 2020. https://threadreaderapp.com/thread/1271948968772030464.html.

La Chapelle, Peter. *I'd Fight the World: A Political History of Old-Time, Hillbilly, and Country Music*. Chicago: University of Chicago Press, 2019.

Lisanby, Sarah H., Jill H. Maddox, Joan Prudic, D. P. Devanand, and Harold A. Sackheim. "The Effects of Electroconvulsive Therapy on Memory of Autobiographical and Public Events." *Archives of General Psychiatry* 57, no. 6 (2000): 581–590. https://jamanetwork.com/journals/jamapsychiatry /article-abstract/481613.

Lynn, Loretta. *Coal Miner's Daughter*. With George Vecsey. Brentwood, TN: Warner Books, 1976.

Lynn, Loretta. *Still Woman Enough: A Memoir*. With Patsi Bale Cox. New York: Hyperion Books, 2002.

Maines, John. "Burt Reynolds' Gigantic Estate Will Become Million-Dollar Homes." *South Florida Sun Sentinel*, September 7, 2018. https://www.sun -sentinel.com/local/palm-beach/fl-pn-burt-reynolds-estate-20180907 -story.html.

McDonough, Jimmy. *Tammy Wynette: Tragic Country Queen*. New York: Viking, 2010.

McMurran, Kristin, and Dolly Carlisle. "A Battered Tammy Wynette Relives the Macabre Abduction that Nearly Killed Her." *People*, October 23, 1978. https://people.com/archive/a-battered-tammy-wynette-relives-the -macabre-abduction-that-nearly-killed-her-vol-10-no-17/.

"Memorial for Tammy Wynette." CNN, April 9, 1998. Laura Murray, YouTube, July 10, 2014. https://www.youtube.com/watch?v=pz8PN17-QDs.

Miller, Walter C., dir. *Twenty-seventh Annual Country Music Association Awards*. September 29, 1993, CBS.

Moore, Bob. Bob Moore (website). http://www.nashvillesound.net/.

Morris, Edward. "Stay Apart and Shut Up, Judge Tells Lorrie and Sammy." CMT News. November 25, 2003. http://www.cmt.com/news/1480805 /stay-apart-and-shut-up-judge-tells-lorrie-and-sammy/.

Myers, Marc. "The Love Song of Virginia Pugh." *Wall Street Journal*, January 31, 2013. https://www.wsj.com/articles/SB1000142412788732337 52045782 69813829094742.

Nair, Yasmin. "On Kink at Pride." Yasmin Nair (blog), June 8, 2021. https:// yasminnair.com/category/gay-marriage/.

Nash, Alanna. *Behind Closed Doors: Talking with the Legends of Country Music*. Lanham, MD: Cooper Square Press, 2002.

"Nashville Edition." *Hee Haw* Wiki, Fandom. Accessed January 24, 2022. https://heehaw.fandom.com/wiki/Nashville_Edition.

N.C. Review of *Womanhood*, by Tammy Wynette. Recording of Special Merit, *Stereo Review*, October 1978, 136. https://worldradiohistory.com/hd2/IDX -Audio/Archive-Stereo-Review-IDX/IDX/70s/HiFi-Stereo-Review-1978 -10-OCR-Page-0136.pdf#search=%22tammy%20wynette%22.

O'Dell, Cary. "'Stand By Your Man'—Tammy Wynette (1968)." Library of Congress, 2010. https://www.loc.gov/static/programs/national -recording-preservation-board/documents/StandByYourMan.pdf.

Padgett, Stephen. "Years in the Making, *Trio* Comes Together." *Cashbox*, March 3, 1987.

Parton, Dolly, Loretta Lynn, and Tammy Wynette. "Silver Threads and Golden Needles." Video. Deaton-Flanigen Productions, 1993.

Peterson, Richard A. "Class Unconsciousness in Country Music." In *You Wrote My Life: Lyrical Themes in Country Music*, edited by Melton A. McLaurin and Richard A. Peterson. Philadelphia: Gordon and Breach, 1992.

Presnell, Jim. "Country Music Brings Special Luster to Fair." *South Florida Sun Sentinel*, January 24, 1986. https://www.sun-sentinel.com/news/fl-xpm -1986-01-24-8601070157-story.html.

Reynolds, Burt, and Tammy Wynette. Interview (Evening Shade/Country Music), February 18, 1994. Reelin' in the Years Productions, YouTube, March 15, 2021. https://www.youtube.com/watch?v=kgENMo7bACs.

Riese, Randall. *Nashville Babylon: The Uncensored Truth and Private Lives of Country Music's Stars*. New York: Congdon and Weed, 1988.

Ronstadt, Linda. *Simple Dreams: A Musical Memoir*. New York: Simon and Schuster Audio, 2015.

Sangalang, Jennifer. "Burt Reynolds and His Many Ties to Florida." *Florida Today*, September 6, 2018. https://www.floridatoday.com/story/news /2018/09/06/burt-reynolds-florida/1215362002/.

"'Segregation Forever': A Fiery Pledge Forgiven, but Not Forgotten." *All*

Things Considered, NPR, January 10, 2013. https://www.npr.org/2013/01 /14/169080969/segregation-forever-a-fiery-pledge-forgiven-but-not -forgotten.

Sesame Street. Season 5, episode 558, "Johnny Cash Visits." December 19, 1973, PBS.

"The Sexes: Total Fascination." *Time*, March 10, 1973.

Shores, Del, dir. *Sordid Lives*. Daly-Harris Productions, Davis Entertainment Classics, Sordid Lives LLC, 2000.

"Sisters in Country: Dolly, Linda and Emmylou." BBC Four, November 4, 2016. Cal Vid, YouTube, July 6, 2019. https://www.youtube.com/watch ?v=uQ7StOs2xY0.

Smarsh, Sarah. *She Come By It Natural: Dolly Parton and the Women Who Lived Her Songs*. New York: Scribner, 2020.

"Spade Cooley Indicted in Murder of His Wife." *Los Angeles Times*, April 26, 1961, 2.

"Stand By Your Man." Grammy Hall of Fame, Recording Academy. Accessed August 5, 2022. https://www.grammy.com/awards/hall-of-fame#s.

"Suit over Wynette's Death Resolved." *Billboard*, April 19, 2002. https://www .billboard.com/music/music-news/suit-over-wynettes-death-resolved -76046/.

"Tammy vs. Tabloids." CMT News. July 23, 2003 (orig. date unknown). http:// www.cmt.com/news/1474555/tammy-vs-tabloids/.

"Tammy Wynette, Artist." Grammy Awards, Recording Academy. Accessed January 21, 2022. https://www.grammy.com/grammys/artists/tammy -wynette/8086.

"Tammy Wynette Bio." Tammy Wynette (website). Accessed August 31, 2022. https://tammywynette.com/about/.

"Tammy Wynette: Burt Reynolds Theatre (Jupiter, FL)." Live performance, January 17, 1983. Wolfgang's. https://www.wolfgangs.com/music/tammy -wynette/audio/20052222-6999.html?tid=29011.

"Tammy Wynette Exhumed." *People*, March 19, 1999. https://people.com /celebrity/tammy-wynette-exhumed/.

"Tammy Wynette — Final Opry Appearance (with Lorrie Morgan)." Dailymotion. 2015. https://www.dailymotion.com/video/x2mzvfn.

"Tammy Wynette Sues Supermarket Tabloids." *Chicago Tribune*, February 26, 1997. https://www.chicagotribune.com/news/ct-xpm-1997-02-26 -9702260034-story.html.

"Tammy Wynette: The 'Tragic Country Queen.'" *Weekend Edition Sunday*, NPR, March 14, 2010. https://www.npr.org/2010/03/14/124540180/tammy -wynette-the-tragic-country-queen.

Thompson, Gayle. "Chris Cagle Not Guilty in Domestic Violence Charge."

The Boot. July 24, 2008. https://theboot.com/chris-cagle-not-guilty-in -domestic-violence-charge/.

Tosches, Nick. *Country: The Twisted Roots of Rock 'n' Roll*. Boston: Da Capo, 1977.

Tosches, Nick. "The Devil in George Jones." *Texas Monthly*, April 26, 2013 (orig. July 1994). https://www.texasmonthly.com/arts-entertainment/the -devil-in-george-jones/.

Trow, George W. S. "Two Musical Gatherings." Talk of the Town, *New Yorker*, April 14, 1973.

Tyson, Timothy B. *The Blood of Emmett Till*. New York: Simon and Schuster, 2017.

Unterberger, Richie. "Jack Rhodes Biography." AllMusic. Accessed January 24, 2022. https://www.allmusic.com/artist/jack-rhodes-mn0000125414 /biography.

Whitburn, Joel. *The* Billboard *Book of Top 40 Country Hits*. Rev. ed. New York: Billboard Books, 2006.

Whitburn, Joel. *Hot Country Songs 1944 to 2008*. Menomonee Falls, WI: Record Research, 2009.

The Wilburn Brothers Show. Season 6, WB-316, "Tammy Wynette." Taped January 14, 1969. Classic TV Archive. http://ctva.biz/US/MusicVariety /WilburnBrothersShow_06_(1968-69).htm.

Wilson, Claire. "Tammy Wynette." Encyclopedia of Alabama. November 4, 2019. http://encyclopediaofalabama.org/article/h-4151.

Wood, Gerry. *Tales from Country Music*. With Paul Zamek. Champaign, IL: Sports Publishing, 2003.

Wynette, Tammy. *Stand By Your Man: An Autobiography*. With Joan Dew. New York: Simon and Schuster, 1979.

"Wynette Autopsy Finds Heart Failure Cause of Death." CNN, Entertainment: Music. May 20, 1999. http://edition.cnn.com/SHOWBIZ/Music/9905/20 /wynette.autopsy/index.html.

"Wynette's Death Questioned." CMT News. July 21, 2003 (orig. date unknown). http://www.cmt.com/news/1474411/wynettes-death -questioned/.

Zaleski, Annie. "Forty-three Years Ago: Tammy Wynette Reportedly Abducted in Nashville." The Boot. Updated October 4, 2021. https:// theboot.com/tammy-wynette-abduction/.

Zibart, Eve. "Tammy on a Tightrope." *Washington Post*, October 26, 1978. https://www.washingtonpost.com/archive/lifestyle/1978/10/26/tammy -on-a-tightrope/d8786a54-9ad8-4924-a1e8-6a943b368b07/.